LIFE TOUCHED WITH WONDER

LIFE TOUCHED WITH WONDER

The SPIRIT of COURAGE

FROM THE EDITORS OF READER'S DIGEST

THE READER'S DIGEST ASSOCIATION, INC.
PLEASANTVILLE, NEW YORK

CONTENTS

LIFE TOUCHED
WITH WONDER

Men wonder at the height of mountains, the huge waves of the sea, the broad flow of rivers, the course of the stars—and forget to wonder at themselves.
— *St. Augustine*

We feel awe when we see a grand landscape or view the majesty of a starry sky. But there's also wonder in a child's kiss when you're feeling down, in a friend's unexpected recovery from a frightening illness, in a walk on a hushed, snowy night. Such moments take us by surprise and lift us from the mundane and the familiar. Suddenly, inexplicably, we catch a glimpse of a reality beyond ourselves, and see evidence that there is something beautiful, merciful, loving knit into the fabric of creation — even in ourselves.

In fact, ordinary people can be the most gifted messengers of wonder. Their stories offer compelling evidence of the power of the spirit in daily life. In this new book series we have selected the best of such true-life stories and present them in separate volumes organized around themes, including hope, love, courage and healing.

This book, *The Spirit of Courage,* celebrates people who found secret strength and prevailed over the sort of difficulties we all face. Their stories will lift your spirit and fortify your soul. Their examples might even change your life.

BILL PORTER:
PROFILE OF COURAGE

BY
TOM HALLMAN, JR.

The alarm rings and Bill Porter stirs. It's 5:45 a.m. The weatherman is predicting rain. With a disability that can cause him considerable pain, he could linger under the covers. People would understand. He knows that.

A surgeon's scar cuts a swath across his back. The medicines littering his night stand offer help, but no cure. The fingers on his right hand are so twisted that he can't tie his shoes. Some days, days like this one, he feels like surrendering. But his dead mother's challenge reverberates in his soul. So, too, do the voices of those who believed him stupid or retarded, incapable of being more than a ward of the state. All his life, he's struggled to prove them wrong. He will not quit.

And so, Bill Porter rises and begins again his fight for independence and dignity.

With trembling hands, the 64-year-old door-to-door salesman dresses carefully: dark slacks with matching blazer, blue shirt, tan raincoat and pinched-front fedora. Image, he believes, is everything.

On the 7:45 bus, he finds a seat in the middle of a pack of teen-agers. He senses the stares. He looks at a boy next to him and smiles. The kid turns away and makes a face at a buddy.

Porter looks at the floor. His face reveals nothing. In his heart, though, he knows he should have been like these kids. He's not angry. His mother had explained how the delivery had been difficult, how the doctor had used an instrument that crushed a section of his brain and caused cerebral palsy, which affects his speech, hands and walk.

At age 13, Bill Porter moved to Portland, Ore., after his father, a salesman, was transferred there. In high school, he was placed in a class for slow kids.

But he wasn't slow.

His mind was trapped in a body that did not work. Speaking was laborious, as if words had to be pulled from a tar pit. People were impatient and didn't listen. He felt different—was different. People like him were considered retarded then. What could his future be?

Porter asked the Vocational Rehabilitation Division for help. They sent him to several social-service agencies, but they called him "unemployable" and said he should collect government disability checks for the rest of his life.

His mother was certain, though, that he could rise above his limitations. Porter wanted to be a salesman. He applied for a job with the Fuller Brush Co., only to be turned down. He couldn't carry a product briefcase or walk a route, they said. When Porter saw a help-wanted ad for Watkins, a company that sold household products door-to-door, his mother set up a meeting. The representative said no, but Porter wouldn't listen. He just wanted a chance. The man relented and offered Porter a section of the city that no other salesman wanted.

It took Porter four false starts before he found the courage to ring the first doorbell. The man who answered told him to go away, a pattern repeated throughout the day.

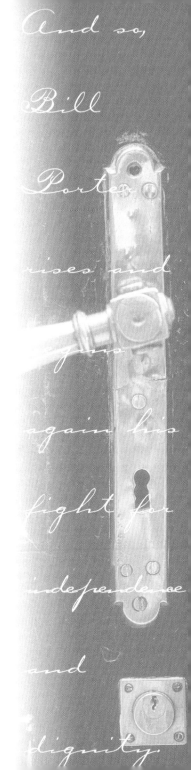

That night, Porter read through company literature and discovered that the products were guaranteed. He would sell that pledge. He just needed people to listen.

If customers turned him down, Porter kept coming back. And he sold. His parents made deliveries because he couldn't drive. He was rewarded with a better territory. For several years, he was Watkins' top retail salesman in a four-state area. Today, he is the only one of the company's 75,000 salespeople who sells door-to-door.

The bus stops and Porter shuffles off. His body is not made for walking. Each step strains his joints. Migraines and other aches often plague him. His right arm is nearly useless. His torso tilts at the waist; he seems to be heading into a strong, steady wind that keeps him off-balance. At times, he looks like a toddler taking his first steps.

He walks eight miles or more a day—every working day.

His first stop today, like every day, is a shoeshine stand where an employee ties his laces. Twice a week, he pays for a shine. At a nearby hotel, a doorman buttons Porter's top shirt button and slips on his clip-on tie. He then walks to another bus that drops him off a mile from his territory. He left home nearly two hours ago.

At the first house, he rings the bell. A woman answers.

"Hello."

"No, thank you, I'm just preparing to leave."

Porter nods. "May I come back later?"

"No."

She shuts the door. Porter's eyes reveal nothing. He moves to the next house. The door opens, then closes. He doesn't get a chance to speak. Porter's expression never changes. He stops at every home in his territory. No doesn't mean never. Some of his best customers are people who repeatedly turned him down before buying. He makes his way down the street.

"I don't want to try it."

"Maybe next time."

"I'm sorry. I'm on the phone."

He makes his way up and down the hills. His briefcase is heavy. His hand hurts. He catches his breath. He walks on.

Ninety minutes later, Porter still has not made a sale. But there is always another home. He walks on.

He knocks on a door. A woman wanders out from the back yard where she's gardening. She often buys, but not today.

"Are you sure?" Porter asks.

She pauses. "Well..."

That's all Porter needs. He walks as fast as he can, tailing her as she heads to the back yard. He sets his briefcase on a bench and opens it. He puts on his glasses, removes his brochures and begins his spiel, showing the woman pictures and describing each product.

"Spices?" "No." "Vanilla?" "No." "Pasta toppings?" "No." "Potpourri?" "No. Maybe nothing today, Bill."

Porter's hearing is the one perfect thing his body does. Except when he gets a live one. Then the word *no* does not register.

"Pepper?" "No." "Laundry soap?" "Hmm." Porter stops. He's a shark smelling blood. He quickly remembers her last order.

"Say, aren't you about out of soap? That's what you bought last time. You ought to be out right about now."

"You're right, Bill. I'll take some."

Because he has difficulty holding a pen, Porter asks his customers to complete their order forms. The woman writes him a check, which he deposits in his briefcase.

Then he is on his way.

No sale.

No sale.

No sale.

Finally, a woman and her daughter invite Porter inside. After a few minutes of small talk, out come the glasses and the brochures.

The woman buys $33 worth of products. Porter pulls on his coat, replaces his hat and follows the woman to the front door. He turns to her, struggling to get out one final sentence. "And I thank you."

He arrives home, in a rainstorm, after 7 p.m. Today was not profitable. He tells himself not to worry. Four days left in the week. At least he's off his feet and home. He and his parents moved here more than 50 years ago. Not a day goes by that he doesn't silently thank them. After his father died, his mother lived off a small pension with help from Porter's income. When she died, she left only the house and a voice he still hears.

Inside, an era is preserved. The telephone is a heavy rotary model. There is no VCR, no cable. He leads a solitary life. Most of his human contact comes on the job. Alone, he does paperwork, reads and watches television, especially sports.

As his frozen dinner warms, he opens his briefcase and stacks the order forms. In two weeks, he will use a manual typewriter to write detailed directions to each house so the woman he hires to make deliveries won't get lost. He can use only one finger and one hand to type.

The job takes him ten hours.

He peddles his goods in downpours, snowstorms and sweltering heat. He does not know how much longer his body can take the pounding. In quieter moments, he wonders if the day is fast approaching when the world will no longer answer his knock at the door. At many homes, the woman of the house is off working. And people

> *The greatest test of courage on earth is to bear defeat without losing heart.*
>
> ROBERT G. INGERSOLL

who are there would often rather buy in bulk at superstores than deal with a stranger who talks about money-back guarantees.

Porter works on straight commission. He gets no paid holidays, vacations or raises. In 1993 he needed back surgery to relieve pain caused by decades of walking. He was laid up for five months and couldn't work. He had to sell his house to pay his debts. He didn't feel sorry for himself. A house is only a building, a place to live, nothing more. He started over again. The new owners froze his rent and agreed to let him live there until he dies. He pays for his medical insurance, a gardener, and a woman to shop for him, clean his house and do his laundry.

He types in the recipient's name on each check and signs his name. The signature is unreadable. But he knows.

Bill Porter.

Bill Porter, salesman.

From his easy chair, Porter hears the wind lash his house. He's sleepy. With great care, he climbs the stairs to his bedroom. Morning will be here soon.

"PLEASE DON'T LEAVE ME!"

BY
JAMES HUTCHISON

*B*uddy Marsh, a truck driver for 40 years, steered his gasoline tanker down the busy road leading to New Zealand's biggest shopping mall, in South Auckland. The 39-ton truck and trailer held more than 8700 gallons of gasoline. It was Thursday evening, August 9, 1990.

As the rig neared the mall, a taxi left the parking lot and pulled out, partially blocking Marsh's lane. He swung away, and a glance in his mirrors showed his trailer just clearing the taxi. Looking ahead again, he gasped in horror. A stopped car lay directly in his path.

Marsh spun the steering wheel and hit the air brakes. Too late. The truck slammed into the rear of the car, spinning it around and rupturing its fuel tank. Gasoline sprayed both vehicles and instantly ignited. The trailer jackknifed and toppled onto the car.

Marsh radioed his shift mate. "Brian, I've had an accident! I'm on fire. Call the emergency services!" He jumped from his cab and ran toward the car, which lay beneath the overturned trailer, flames licking upward. Worse, fuel was spewing out of a hole in the trailer. *The whole rig could blow!*

"Let's go, mum!" Shirley Young begged her mother, Gaylene. It was Thursday — the late shopping night at Manukau City Centre mall. For the 12-year-old, this was a highlight of the week. So her mother grabbed her car keys, and they were on their way.

As they approached the mall, Gaylene pulled over to the curb and dropped Shirley off. "Wait, Mum," she said. "My money . . ." Opening the passenger door, Shirley leaned in to tell her mother that she had forgotten her purse and would have to go back home to get it.

One second Gaylene Young was talking with her daughter; the next, she was whirling around in a vortex of crumpling metal. Flames poured into the car. *Where is Shirley?* Gaylene thought frantically. A sudden, excruciating pain shot up her legs — her clothes were burning. She tried to open the buckled doors. "No!" she screamed. "I won't die like this!"

Marsh got to the car just as a bystander, David Petera, hauled Gaylene out and used his body to smother the flames on her. Above the roar of the fire, Marsh heard a voice calling, "Mum, Mum!" He searched beneath the toppled trailer and saw a dark-haired girl trapped in a tiny space between a rear wheel and the chassis.

Marsh took Shirley beneath the arms, but he couldn't budge her. The wheel assembly had pinned her lower body to the ground. Petera crawled in alongside. Through a gap in the chassis Marsh could see a stream of fuel spilling from the trailer into the gutter. "We've got to get her out *now!*" he shouted to Petera.

Marsh dashed back to the burning cab and twisted the ignition key. The engine roared to life. He inched the rig forward, but Shirley shrieked in pain. "It's no good," Petera called. "She's still trapped."

A wall of fire ran the entire length of the tanker, threatening to sweep under the trailer where Shirley lay. Marsh grabbed an extinguisher from the truck's cab and sprayed around the girl, hoping to buy precious seconds.

9

Then came a thunderous boom as an explosion blew a hole in one of the trailer's four fuel compartments. Marsh and Petera, shielded from the full force of the blast by the trailer's chassis, staggered out into the open. A policeman ordered them away. Truck, trailer and car were now lost behind flames shooting 100 yards into the air.

"That poor girl," Marsh said. "She didn't have a chance."

Sirens blaring, two fire engines from Manukau Station arrived. The heat was so intense that one of the first firefighters on the scene, Royd Kennedy, saw his boots, fireproof trousers and the rubber on his breath-

ing apparatus begin to singe. When he and his part-ner, Mike Keys, turned a hose on the fire, the water just turned to steam.

Uppermost in the firefighters' minds was the knowledge that tankers can blow up in a giant fuel and air-vapor conflagration reaching outward for hundreds of yards. About 20,000 shoppers were packed into the mall that night, just 100 yards from the burning truck.

More fire crews arrived and concentrated on using the streams of water from their hoses to try to push the flames away from the tanker. But more explosions from the trailer forced Kennedy and the others back.

As they prepared for another assault on the fire, a high-pitched wail cut through the night. One firefighter dismissed it as expanding metal. When the eerie sound came again, it raised the hair on Kennedy's neck. *It's coming from the tanker!* he thought. Shielding his eyes, he peered into the wall of flames. For a split second they parted. Beneath the trailer he saw something waving — a child's hand.

"Cover me!" Kennedy shouted and ran straight into the inferno.

For ten minutes Shirley had been roasting in a sea of fire, crying for help. She was giddy with pain and gasoline fumes, and her mind began to drift. She had a sudden, vivid image of her grandfather, Edward Young, and her great-uncle, Vincent Bidios. Both had died years before, but she clearly recognized them. *They're guardian angels now. They'll watch over me.* The thought gave her new strength. Straining to see through the flames, Shirley glimpsed moving figures. Then, with every ounce of force she had, she screamed.

As Kennedy neared the blaze, the heat hit him like a physical blow, stinging his face through his visor. Under the trailer, he found Shirley clutching an overhead brake cable. Her hips and thighs were under the wheel assembly, and her legs were twisted up like a grasshopper's next to her chest.

"I'm scared!" Shirley wailed. "Please don't leave me!"

"I promise you I won't," Kennedy said, looking into her trusting eyes. "We're in this together now, so we have to help each other." He cradled her body in his arms. The trailer was still shielding them from the main blaze, but the air was so thick with gasoline fumes that the two could barely breathe.

Whoosh! The vapor suddenly ignited, and the air exploded around them. *This is it,* Kennedy thought. *We're goners.* He felt sick with helplessness as flames washed over the girl. For a moment the fire drew back. Unstrapping his helmet, he said to Shirley, "Put this on." He tightened the strap under her chin and flipped down the visor.

A second wave of fire washed over them. This time the helmet gave Shirley's head some protection. But more explosions rocked the trailer. Kennedy looked down at the girl's tortured body. *I won't leave you. I promise.* He wrapped his arms tightly around her and waited for the final surge of flame that would surely immolate them both.

Instead there came a sudden ice-cold waterfall. "My mates are here!" Kennedy yelled.

Four hoses were directed onto Kennedy and Shirley, and 1200 gallons of freezing water were now cascading over them each minute. Ironically, the two began to shiver violently. They were in the first stages of hypothermia.

"We'll get someone to relieve you," a fireman yelled to Kennedy.

"No," he said firmly. "I must stay with her. I promised."

Grant Pennycook, a paramedic from a waiting ambulance crew, donned a bunker coat and helmet and, biting back his fear, headed into the flames. As he crawled to where Shirley and Kennedy lay, he saw there was no room to get an I.V. drip going. Coming back out, he radioed the trauma team assembling at Middlemore Hospital. "Prepare for a patient with critical burns, fractures and crushing to her lower body." Trauma victims need to get to a hospital within an hour of injury — the so-called golden hour — to have a decent chance of survival. Shirley had been under the tanker for over 30 minutes.

Kennedy kept talking to keep her conscious. "What do you watch on TV?" he asked. They spoke about her favorite shows. *This man's so brave,* Shirley told herself. *He could get out of here any time he wants.* She thought again of her guardian angels. *Granddad and Uncle Vincent must have sent him.*

Occasionally she would let out stifled moans. "It's okay — yell all you want," Kennedy encouraged. The pain was becoming unbearable. She cried out, pulling hard on his thick hair in her agony. But she never shed tears.

The flow of water faltered for an instant, and flames rolled in. When the water came pouring back, Kennedy was horrified to see several layers of skin on Shirley's arms slide down around her wrists. She was also growing visibly weaker.

"Do you like horses?" he asked, desperate to keep her talking.

"I've never been on a horse."

"When we get out of here, I promise you a ride on my daughter's horse."

As Kennedy talked, he kept checking Shirley's pulse. She'd been trapped for nearly 40 minutes. *Dear God, how much more can she take?*

Suddenly he felt Shirley's pulse flutter, and she closed her eyes. "Shirley, talk to me!" he pleaded. She rallied briefly, lifted her head and looked into his eyes. "If I don't make it, tell Mum I love her," she whispered. Her head lolled back in his arms.

"We're losing her!" he yelled. "Throw me an Air Viva!" He put the mask of the portable resuscitator over her face and forced air into her lungs. She opened her eyes.

"You tell your mum yourself that you love her," he scolded. "I promised I wouldn't leave you. Now don't you leave me!"

Keep your fears to yourself, but share your courage.

ROBERT LOUIS STEVENSON

The desperate rescue team had brought in air bags to elevate the trailer. Made of rubber reinforced with steel, the bags could lift a railroad boxcar two feet — more than enough to slip the girl out. They slid one under each set of rear wheels and pumped in air. But the ground was sodden from all the water, and one of the air bags was sinking into the mud. Praying for the inches they needed, the rescue team shoved a small hydraulic ram under the chassis. The trailer rose slightly. It would have to be enough.

Kennedy gently untangled Shirley's legs from under the wheel. They were crushed so badly that they were like jelly in his hands. Soon her crumpled body was loose from its prison.

We're free! As Kennedy carried her to a stretcher, she smiled weakly at him, and he kissed her on the cheek. "You've done it, Shirley," he said. Then, overcome by fumes, shock and cold, he pitched forward into the arms of another firefighter.

Firemen were at last pouring foam onto the tanker. Any earlier, and it would have endangered Kennedy and the girl. The flames were quenched in minutes.

When Kennedy's station officer, John Hyland, returned to the scene the next morning, he saw something that will haunt him for the rest of his life. For 70 yards, the top layer of asphalt had been melted away in the inferno, in one section down six inches to bare gravel — except for a patch about as big as a kitchen table, so lightly scorched by fire that a painted line was still visible. It was where Shirley had been lying. "It was as if the devil was determined to take that girl," one firefighter said, "and when she was snatched away, he just gave up."

Middlemore orthopedic surgeons set Shirley's fractures and implanted a pin in her crushed right leg. Burn specialists saved what they could of the charred flesh on her legs. But the shock to her young body had been massive. "She may not pull through," the family was told.

For two weeks Shirley lay in intensive care, sometimes heavily sedated. Hooked to a respirator, she couldn't talk. On the fourth morning, as she drifted in and out of sleep, she scrawled a note: "I love you, Mummy." The next day they wheeled Gaylene into Shirley's ward, and mother and daughter wept with happiness.

Shirley's calf muscle was so severely damaged that her right leg had to be amputated below the knee. She took the news bravely.

Despite an unwritten rule that firefighters should never visit victims — to guard against becoming too emotional on the job — Kennedy visited Shirley often, eating her chocolates and clowning with her. "This kid is far too noisy," he scribbled on her chart.

"She's a miracle child," Kennedy says. "No one knows how she survived in there."

But Shirley knows: "I had a guardian angel watching over me."

What would life be if we had

no courage to attempt anything?

VINCENT VAN GOGH

THE POWER OF MY POWERLESS BROTHER

BY

CHRISTOPHER DE VINCK

In the house where I grew up, my brother was on his back in his bed for almost 33 years, in the same corner of his room, under the same window, beside the same yellow walls. Oliver was blind and mute. His legs were twisted. He didn't have the strength to lift his head or the intelligence to learn anything.

Today I am an English teacher, and each time I introduce my class to *The Miracle Worker*, a play about the blind and deaf Helen Keller, I tell my students about Oliver. Once a boy raised his hand and said, "Oh, Mr. de Vinck, you mean he was a vegetable."

I stammered for a few seconds. My family and I fed Oliver. We changed his diapers, bathed him, tickled his chest to make him laugh. We listened to him laugh as we watched television downstairs. We listened to him as he rocked his arms up and down to make the bed squeak. We listened to him cough in the middle of the night.

"Well, I guess you could call him a vegetable," I finally said. "I called him Oliver, my brother. You would have liked him."

When my mother was pregnant with Oliver, she was overcome by fumes from a leaking coal-burning stove. My father pulled her outside, where she revived quickly.

On April 20, 1947, Oliver was born. A healthy-looking, plump, beautiful boy. A few months later, my mother brought him to a window and held him in the sunlight. Oliver looked directly into the sun and my mother realized that her baby was blind. My parents learned, with the passing months, that blindness was only part of the problem.

The doctor at Mt. Sinai Hospital in New York City told my mother and father there was absolutely nothing that could be done for Oliver. He didn't want my parents to grasp at false hope. "You could place him in an institution," he said.

"But he is our son," my parents replied. "We will take Oliver home, of course."

The good doctor answered, "Then take him home and love him."

We'd wrap a box of baby cereal for Oliver at Christmas and place it under the tree. We'd pat his head with a damp cloth in the middle of a July heat wave. His baptismal certificate hung on the wall above his head. A bishop came to the house and confirmed him.

Even now, five years after his death, Oliver remains the weakest, most helpless human being I ever met, and yet he was one of the most powerful. He could do absolutely nothing except breathe, sleep and eat; yet he was responsible for love, courage and insight.

When I was small my mother would say, "Isn't it wonderful that you can see?" Once she said, "When you go to heaven, Oliver will run to you and embrace you. And he will say, 'Thank you.'" I remember, too, that my mother explained how we were blessed with Oliver in ways that were not clear to her at first.

So often parents are faced with the problem of a severely retarded child who is also hyperactive, demanding or wild, who needs constant care. So many people have little choice but to place their child in an institution.

We were fortunate that Oliver didn't need us to be in his room all day. He never knew what his condition was. We were blessed with his presence, a true presence of peace.

When I was in my early 20s I met a girl and fell in love. After a few months I brought her home to meet my family. When my mother went to the kitchen to prepare dinner, I asked the girl, "Would you like to see Oliver?"

"No," she answered.

Soon after, I met Roe and brought her home to meet my family. When it was time for me to feed Oliver, I sheepishly asked Roe if she'd like to see him.

"Sure," she said.

I sat at Oliver's bedside and gave him his first spoonful, his second. "Can I do that?" Roe asked with ease, with freedom, with compassion. So I gave her the bowl and she fed Oliver.

The power of the powerless. Which woman would you marry? Today Roe and I have three children.

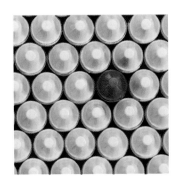

To go against the dominant thinking

of your friends, of most of the

people you see every day, is perhaps

the most difficult act of heroism you

can perform.

THEODORE H. WHITE

THE COURAGE OF SAM BIRD

BY
B.T. COLLINS

I met Capt. Samuel R. Bird on a dusty road near An Khe, South Vietnam, one hot July day in 1966. I was an artillery forward observer with Bravo Company, 2nd/12th Cavalry, 1st Cavalry Division, and I looked it. I was filthy, sweaty, and jaded by war, and I thought, *Oh, brother, get a load of this.* Dressed in crisply starched fatigues, Captain Bird was what we called "squared away"—ramrod straight, eyes on the horizon. Hell, you could still see the shine on his boot tips beneath the road dust.

After graduation from Officer Candidate School, I had sought adventure by volunteering for Vietnam. But by that hot and dangerous July, I was overdosed on "adventure," keenly interested in survival and very fond of large rocks and deep holes. Bird was my fourth company commander, and my expectations were somewhat cynical when he called all his officers and sergeants together.

"I understand this company has been in Vietnam almost a year and has never had a party," he said.

Now, we officers and sergeants had our little clubs to which we repaired. So we stole bewildered looks at one another, cleared our throats and wondered what this wiry newcomer was talking about.

"The men are going to have a party," he announced, "and they're not going to pay for it. Do I make myself clear?"

A party for the "grunts" was the first order of business! Sam Bird had indeed made himself clear. We all chipped in to get food and beer for about 160 men. The troops were surprised almost to the point of suspicion—who, after all, had ever done anything for them? But that little beer and bull session was exactly what those war-weary men needed. Its effect on morale was profound. I began to watch our new captain more closely.

Bird and I were the same age, 26, but eons apart in everything else. He was from the sunny heartland of Kansas, I from the suburbs of New York City. He prayed every day and was close to his God. My faith had evaporated somewhere this side of altar boy. I was a college dropout who had wandered into the Army with the words "discipline problem" close on my heels. He had graduated from The Citadel, South Carolina's proud old military school.

If ever a man looked like a leader, it was Sam Bird. He was tall and lean, with penetrating blue eyes. But the tedium and terror of a combat zone take far sterner qualities than mere appearance.

Our outfit was helicoptered to a mountain outpost one day for the thankless task of preparing a position for others to occupy. We dug trenches, filled sandbags, strung wire under a blistering sun. It was hard work, and Sam was everywhere, pitching in with the men. A colonel who was supposed to oversee the operation remained at a shelter, doing paper work. Sam looked at what his troops had accomplished, then, red-faced, strode over to the colonel's sanctuary. We couldn't hear what he was saying to his superior, but we had the unmistakable sense that Sam was uncoiling a bit. The colonel suddenly found time to inspect the fortifications and thank the men for a job well done.

Another day, this time on the front lines after weeks of awful chow, we were given something called "coffee cake" that had the look and texture of asphalt paving. Furious, Sam got on the radio phone to headquarters. He reached the colonel and said, "Sir, you and the supply officer need to come out here and taste the food, because this rifle company is not taking one step further." *Not a good way to move up in the Army,* I thought. But the colonel came out, and the food improved from that moment. Such incidents were not lost on the men of Bravo Company.

During the monsoon season we had to occupy a landing zone. The torrential, wind-driven rains had been falling for weeks. Like everyone else I sat under my poncho in a stupor, wondering how much of the wetness was rainwater and how much was sweat. Nobody cared that the position was becoming flooded. We had all just crawled inside ourselves. Suddenly I saw Sam, Mr. Spit and Polish, with nothing on but his olive-drab undershorts and his boots. He was digging a drainage ditch down the center of the camp. He didn't say anything, just dug away, mud spattering his chest, steam rising from his back and shoulders. Slowly and sheepishly we emerged from under our ponchos, and shovels in hand, we began helping "the old man" get the ditch dug. We got the camp tolerably dried out and with that one simple act transformed our morale.

Sam deeply loved the U.S. Army, its history and traditions. Few of the men knew it, but he had been in charge of a special honors unit of the Old Guard, which serves at the Tomb of the Unknown Soldier in Arlington National Cemetery and participates in the Army's most solemn ceremonies. He was the kind of guy whose eyes would mist during the singing of the National Anthem.

Sam figured patriotism was just a natural part of being an American. But he knew that morale was a function not so much of inspiration as of good boots, dry socks, extra ammo and hot meals.

Sam's philosophy was to put his troops first. On that foundation he built respect a brick at a time. His men ate first; he ate last. Instead of merely learning their names, he made it a point to know the men. A lot of the soldiers were high-school dropouts and would-be tough guys just a few years younger than himself. Some were scared, and a few were still in partial shock at being in a shooting war. Sam patiently worked on their pride and self-confidence. Yet there was never any doubt who was in charge. I had been around enough to know what a delicate accomplishment that was.

Half in wonder, an officer once told me, "Sam can dress a man down till his ears burn, and the next minute that same guy is eager to follow him into hell." But he never chewed out a man in front of his subordinates.

Sam wouldn't ask his men to do anything he wasn't willing to do himself. He dug his own foxholes. He never gave lectures on appearance, but even at God-forsaken outposts in the Central Highlands, he would set aside a few ounces of water from his canteen to shave. His uniform, even if it was jungle fatigues, would be as clean and neat as he could make it. Soon all of Bravo Company had a reputation for looking sharp.

One sultry and miserable day on a dirt road at the base camp, Sam gathered the men together and began talking about how tough the infantryman's job is, how proud he was of them, how they should always look out for each other. He took out a bunch of Combat Infantryman's Badges, signifying that a soldier has paid his dues under fire, and he pre-

Courage is almost a contradiction in terms. It means a strong desire to live, taking the form of a readiness to die.

G. K. CHESTERTON

sented one to each of the men. There wasn't a soldier there who would have traded that moment on the road for some parade-ground ceremony.

That was the way Sam Bird taught me leadership. He packed a lot of lessons into the six months we served together. Put the troops first. Know that morale often depends on small things. Respect every person's dignity. Always be ready to fight for your people. Lead by example. Reward performance. But Sam had another lesson to teach, one that would take long and painful years, a lesson in courage.

I left Bravo Company in December 1966 to return to the States for a month before joining a Special Forces unit. Being a big, tough paratrooper, I didn't tell Sam what his example had meant to me. But I made a point of visiting his parents and sister in Wichita, Kan., just before Christmas to tell them how much he'd affected my life, and how his troops would walk off a cliff for him. His family was relieved when I told them that his tour of combat was almost over and he'd be moving to a safe job in the rear.

Two months later, in a thatched hut in the Mekong Delta, I got a letter from Sam's sister, saying that he had conned his commanding officer into letting him stay an extra month with his beloved Bravo Company. On his last day, January 27, 1967—his 27th birthday—the men had secretly planned a party, even arranging to have a cake flown in. They were going to "pay back the old man." But orders came down for Bravo to lead an airborne assault on a North Vietnamese regimental headquarters.

Sam's helicopter was about to touch down at the attack point when it was ripped by enemy fire. Slugs shattered his left ankle and right leg. Another struck the left side of his head, carrying off almost a quarter of his skull. His executive officer, Lt. Dean Parker, scooped Sam's brains back into the gaping wound.

Reading the letter, I felt as if I'd been kicked in the stomach. I began querying every hospital in Vietnam to find out if Sam was still alive. But in June, before I could discover his fate, I was in a firefight in an enemy-controlled zone. I had thrown four grenades. The fifth one exploded in my hand. I lost an arm and a leg.

Nearly a year later, in March 1968, I finally caught up with Sam. I was just getting the hang of walking with an artificial leg when I visited him at the VA Medical Center in Memphis, Tenn. Seeing him, I had to fight back the tears. The wiry, smiling soldier's soldier was blind in the left eye and partially so in the right. Surgeons had removed metal shards and damaged tissue from deep within his brain, and he had been left with a marked depression on the left side of his head. The circles under his eyes told of sleepless hours and great pain.

The old clear voice of command was slower now, labored and with an odd, high pitch. I saw his brow knit as he looked through his one good eye, trying to remember. He recognized me, but believed I had served with him in Korea, his first tour of duty.

Slowly, Sam rebuilt his ability to converse. But while he could recall things from long ago, he couldn't remember what he had eaten for breakfast. Headaches came on him like terrible firestorms. There was pain, too, in his legs. He had only partial use of one arm, with which he'd raise himself in front of the mirror to brush his teeth and shave.

He had the support of a wonderful family, and once he was home in Wichita, his sister brought his old school sweetheart, Annette Blazier, to see him. A courtship began, and in 1972 they married.

They built a house like Sam had dreamed of—red brick, with a flag-pole out front. He had developed the habit of addressing God as "Sir" and spoke to him often. He never asked to be healed. At every table grace, he thanked God for sending him Annette and for "making it possible for me to live at home in a free country."

In 1976, Sam and Annette traveled to The Citadel for his 15th class reunion. World War II hero Gen. Mark Clark, the school's president emeritus, asked about his wounds and said, "On behalf of your country, I want to thank you for all you did."

With pride, Sam answered, "Sir, it was the least I could do."

Later Annette chided him gently for understating the case. After all, he had sacrificed his health and career in Vietnam. Sam gave her an incredulous look. "I had friends who didn't come back," he said. "I'm enjoying the freedoms they died for."

I visited Sam in Wichita and phoned him regularly. You would not have guessed that he lived with pain every day. Once, speaking of me to his sister, he said, "I should never complain about the pain in my leg, because B.T. doesn't have a leg." I'd seen a lot of men with lesser wounds reduced to anger and self-pity. Never a hint of that passed Sam's lips, though I knew that, every waking moment, he was fighting to live.

On October 18, 1984, after 17 years, Sam's body couldn't take any more. When we received the news of his death, a number of us from Bravo Company flew to Wichita, where Sam was to be buried with his forebears.

The day before the burial, his old exec, Dean Parker, and I went to the funeral home to make sure everything was in order. As Dean straightened the brass on Sam's uniform, I held my captain's hand and looked into his face, a face no longer filled with pain. I thought about how unashamed Sam always was to express his love for his country, how sunny and unaffected he was in his devotion to his men. I ached that I had never told him what a fine soldier and man he was. But in my deep sadness I felt a glow of pride for having served with him, and for having learned the lessons of leadership that would serve me all my life. That is why I am telling you about Samuel R. Bird and these things that happened so long ago.

Peace has its victories, but it takes a brave man to win them.

RALPH WALDO EMERSON

Chances are, you have seen Sam Bird. He was the tall officer in charge of the casket detail at the funeral of President John F. Kennedy. Historian William Manchester described him as "a lean, sinewy Kansan, the kind of American youth whom Congressmen dutifully praise each Fourth of July and whose existence many, grown jaded by years on the Hill, secretly doubt."

There can be no doubt about Sam, about who he was, how he lived and how he led. We buried him that fall afternoon, as they say, "with honors." But as I walked from that grave, I knew I was the honored one, for having known him.

Courage is not the towering oak
that sees storms come and go;
it is the fragile blossom
that opens in the snow.

ALICE MACKENZIE SWAIM

THE WOMAN IN THE KITCHEN

BY

GARY ALLEN SLEDGE

My mother looked like a photograph by Dorothea Lange, one of those Depression-era children pinned against a backdrop of bare boards and a denuded landscape. She was fragile-boned, with eyes deep and dark as if bruised by sorrow. Yet I realize today, ten years after her death, what uncommon courage she possessed. What pioneer strength she had to transform a life that others would call ordinary into something wonderful for those of us blessed to call her daughter, sister, wife and mother.

She never let us look down. Though her own life was filled with harsh circumstances, she believed that the future would be better as soundly as she believed in God. She showed us this conviction daily, and yet the earliest tale I heard her tell about herself was of a little girl who had to give up what she loved best. This is the first story in my mother's "Tale of Three Stoves."

"Joanna," her mother said in Hungarian. "You must choose. You can take only one toy with you. There is no room."

The girl is eight, maybe nine, and thin as a waif. She is deliberating with great seriousness. "Yes, Mama."

Her brother and older sister, running in and out of the plain clapboard cabin, are ecstatic because tomorrow the train will take them away from these West Virginia hills forever.

Her brother, John, comes into the kitchen carrying Father's shotgun. He puts it behind the front door so he won't forget it. "Hurry up, little goose," he tells Joanna, who is studying a rag doll and a black cast-iron toy stove.

They are her only real toys, and she loves them dearly. They were bought by her father, one each for the last two Christmases. Now she is allowed only one, because the family is carrying everything they own to California, and will be charged by the weight.

The year is 1929, and the town they are leaving is Monclo. There, a village of Hungarians work in the coal mines at the end of a railroad line, where the train cannot turn around and has to back up to leave.

It is a world I can barely imagine. It is not merely that there was no TV or telephones. Hers was a world of singular things. One pair of shoes, one kind of cereal, one pencil, one school book, one winter coat. It was a world where alternatives were few, choices crucial, and loss a fearful possibility.

"Which one did you choose, Mommy?" I used to ask, even after I knew the story.

"The doll."

"Because you loved it best?"

"No, because the stove was heavier and I was afraid there wouldn't be room for things my mother needed to take. I loved the stove best."

"What did you do with it?"

"The night before we left, we stayed with neighbors, the Demjens. Mary was just my age and my best friend. We used to play together, baking mud pies on my stove. I thought she would take good care of it. So

I gave it to her." Mother held out both hands, re-enacting the mythic transfer.

"And Uncle John left the shotgun behind the door and got a spanking, right?"

"Right."

She told me these and other stories to teach me the survival skills of self-denial, so I would never fear want. But she also fed me Cream of Wheat, cabbage rolls and a wondrous banquet of books and the Bible, so I would never feel empty. Her Biblical hero was Joseph, who rose from the pit to the pinnacle because he learned how to serve.

For three years, while my father was fighting in the Pacific, she raised me alone. It was during this long isolation that she wrote down the story of the stove for her old friend Mary, and as a family keepsake. She wrote with a No. 2 pencil on brown grocery bags because paper was scarce during the war.

When my father returned, he and a couple of other ambitious young men borrowed money to buy a small stand of timber on a range of hills above the Russian River on the northern California coast. Together, they went into logging.

My mother and I went along. It was an ideal situation for a boy of six. We slept in Army-surplus tents and used a two-holer dug behind a thicket of pine. On the opposite side of the camp was a shed where blasting caps and dynamite were stored. I was forever warned to stay away . . . but forever tantalized by the danger. I played under the six-foot circular saw blade, and heard the whack of the ax into the thick hide of redwood, the dying thunder crack of great trees, and the roar of the diesel tractor belching black smoke. But while I climbed trees and played in the rushing stream, my mother cooked for half a dozen lumberjacks on a Coleman stove, carried water up 57 steep steps from the stream for drinking and washing, and pressed work shirts with flatirons heated in wood-fire coals.

I can still see her, a lock of hair loosed from a red kerchief, scrubbing a blackened pot with sand. Or baking potatoes among the pulsing embers in the open pit. Once, my father was paid for an order of redwood with cases of Army-surplus Spam, and for months my mother turned it into breakfast, lunch and dinner in a hundred disguises.

For the four years that they struggled on that ridge, my mother created a magic realm for a child. In the evenings she and I would walk out to the knoll and watch the does bring their fawns to drink at our stream. She supplied the commentary to our lives. "Remember the night the mountain lion jumped over the tent?" "Remember how it rained for a week and the cots sank in the mud?" "Remember when you got tick fever?"

My father had the right idea. California was throwing up tract houses by the thousands. But the larger mills in the area used threats and extortion to run the little ones out of business. It was a plan that was born to fail, I suppose. And with it, to a certain extent, my parents' youthful expectations failed. My father went to work in the postwar factories that grew up along the San Joaquin River. It was an important sacrifice for both of them. It meant the displacement of their dreams to assure a future for me and my newly born brother, Robert. It never occurred to them to duck this responsibility. They did what they had to do. Which brings me to the story of my mother's second stove.

I long to accomplish a great and noble task, but it is my chief duty to accomplish small tasks as if they were great and noble.

HELEN KELLER

One morning mother was cooking outdoors on the Coleman, which sat on a plank table under a tree. The gas tank must have been pumped up too high, because the flames shot several feet in the air. A low-hanging tree limb caught fire. Gasoline must have leaked; the table ignited. A burning branch fell in the dry grass, and the fire spread.

"Get back! Run for help!" she called to me. But I couldn't move. *What if the fire reached the dynamite shed?* I stood there with a cup of water and toothbrush in my hand, feeling cowardly and useless. Mother was 95 pounds dripping wet, but she heaved shovelful after shovelful of dirt on the growing wall of flames. I was afraid the gasoline would explode and she would disappear in a ball of fire. But she kept throwing dirt on the table and stove, and finally the fire went out.

Afterward she came to kiss me on the cheek, marked by dried toothpaste. Only then did her fear and relief express themselves. It was the only time I saw her cry.

When I was old enough to go to school, she and I moved to Antioch while my father stayed on the mountain. She rented two rooms in a tumbledown, century-old house by the river for $10 a month.

There was 50 feet between us and the water, and the Southern Pacific railroad cut right through them. In the late afternoons, we'd take a walk along the tracks. My mother had an abiding love for perspectives. Tops of hills, ocean shores and riverbanks were her natural habitat.

We'd sit on the huge stones of the levee and she'd tell me stories about the freighters churning upriver to Sacramento. Sometimes a crewman would come to the rail and wave. "That man probably breathed the air of China or walked the shores of the Philippines," she'd say, "where there are palm-tree jungles and butterflies big as kites."

Some Sundays we visited my grandmother who lived on the outskirts of town, where the ancient sea-bottom hills rolled up to the flanks of Mount Diablo, one of the highest peaks in the Coast Range. Mother and I would climb the first ridge and look over the town and the San Joaquin Delta.

There was something in her demeanor at such times that said: One day this will be all yours. Since she had little to give me, she gave me the world. It was about that time I began to view her as a forlorn creature, one of those maidens imprisoned in some dark tower, or toiling unobserved in the kitchens of an ignoring patriarch.

I remember her now at a church dinner, with the third stove that marks her story. I was a teen-ager, already making my own way, self-satisfied with my prospects for which she and my father had sacrificed so much. Suddenly I caught one of those glimpses of adult reality that come to the young as a special revelation.

It was a "Church Luau," and the menu was pineapple this and coconut that and egg foo yong. I was a youth representative at the head table, sitting with the pastor and the church leaders. I went into the kitchen to get more to eat. It was jammed with jostling, sweating ladies, and there, working at the hot six-burner stove, was my mother, face steamed and flush, turning a mess of eggs in a long cake pan. Somehow, with that callow reaction known primarily to teen-agers, it embarrassed me to see her toiling away there. I tiptoed back outside.

After dinner, the men and women at the head table had their places cleared, and the minister began his announcements. "First, let's bring out those ladies who made all this possible."

There was a round of applause. A hesitant line of women came out. Mother, last of all, was the tiniest one, standing closest to the door. Again it shocked me to realize that my mother—who was everything in my eyes—was not one of those who sat up front on the dais, but was one who served in the kitchen.

Why was she never rightly rewarded or recognized? I felt a curious mixture of resentment for the leaders and yet a new appreciation for this woman who, all her life, had given herself away. Counting herself not worthy to sit at the head, she served. The minister was more right than he knew; she was, for me, "one of those ladies who made everything possible."

She never had the opportunity to turn her dreams into something entirely her own. Her story was written out on paper bags with a No. 2 pencil, and never saw print. But because of the wealth of imagination she poured into us, my brother and I had the benefit of love, security and the rewards that she and my father squeezed from their livelihood.

I went to college, married and moved to New York. In a very short while, Mother got sick. It was an auto-immune disease. Her liver was rebelling against itself.

A few years before she died, she planned a trip to New York to see us. Then she began to dream. Maybe she could make a bigger trip of it. Go back to West Virginia. It would be the first time in nearly 50 years she would see her native hills. A quick exchange of letters with her old childhood friend Mary Demjen arranged everything.

The reunion completed a circle for my mother. There was cake and coffee, white linen and old silver, and table talk about people and places gone by. The two women lingered, like playmates reluctant to give up their enjoyments in the late-afternoon sun.

As they were about to part, Mary pretended to remember something. She went into the other room and brought out a small box wrapped in white paper.

My mother made small protests, expecting some local memento of this wonderful occasion. But as she unfolded the paper, her hands began to tremble. A shape out of memory revealed itself. A small black stove. It still had the little burner lids and a skillet to cook mud pies.

Father, hear the prayer we offer;

Not for ease that prayer shall be,

But for strength that we may ever

Live our lives courageously.

LOVE M. WILLIS

Her eyes filled with tears, but her face was radiant. "Mary, you didn't forget," she said softly. "It's just as I remembered it. What I always wanted."

"My mother kept it all these years," Mary said graciously. "You *know* how mothers are."

The two grown women cried in one another's arms.

It's difficult to know what counts in this world. Most of us count credits, honors, dollars. But at the bulging center of midlife, I am beginning to see that the things that really matter take place not in the board rooms, but in the kitchens of the world. Memory, imagination, love are some of those things. Service to God and the ones we love is another.

I once asked my mother, "If you could have anything you ever wanted, what would you ask for?"

"Nothing," she said, touching my head in that teasing sort of common benediction mothers give to inquisitive children. "I have you, Rob, Dad. I have everything."

At the time, I didn't believe her. Now I have two children of my own, and I finally know.

I have a mental snapshot: my mother in her last months sitting outside in the sun, her swollen legs propped up on a pillow. Her chair is sinking into the wet grass. Her head, covered with a floppy red hat, is nodding down. But nearby, almost within reach, on the concrete walk which sparkles in the afternoon sun, is a small black stove with little burner lids, and a skillet for cooking mud pies.

My brother, Robert, has it now. It sits in a place of honor, on a shelf in the sun porch of his home in Oakland. It stands for simplicity, courage, grace and service. It stands for the woman in the kitchen.

A veil parts for me. Time turns back upon itself. I see the whole cycle of her life as one dance, one ceremony of kindness and self-sacrifice.

In my mind's eye I see her standing by the door. Don't hold back now, don't cast your dark eyes down. Come out of the kitchen. Come up here to the table, Mother, to the very head.

A DOG LIKE NO OTHER

BY
PETER MUILENBURG

A waning moon had turned the muddy waters of Oyster Creek to quicksilver. Not so much as a zephyr stirred the inlet where our 42-foot ketch *Breath* lay in the delta of western Africa's mighty Gambia River near Banjul, the capital of Gambia. Days before, we'd sailed in off a thousand miles of ocean. Snug in this anchorage, we could still hear surf thundering just beyond the low span of the Denton Bridge.

The chance to see Africa had brought our family back together for a couple of months. Our older son, Rafael, 20, had taken leave from college to join the rest of us: Diego, 13, my wife, Dorothy, and our little black dog, Santos.

Breath had been our only home since I had built the vessel on St. John in the Virgin Islands in the early 1980s. Life afloat had knit close bonds. Everyone had responsibilities—the boys were standing watch when they were six. And for the past eight years, Santos, our loving, feisty, 11-pound schipperke, was at our side.

When we went to bed that night, Santos lay on the cabin top, which he vacated only in the worst weather. He touched his nose to Dorothy's face as she bent low to nuzzle him good-night. His ardent eyes flared briefly—he worshiped her—then he returned to his duty.

We slept easier with him aboard. It was his self-appointed mission to ensure that no one, friend or foe, approached within 100 yards of *Breath* without a warning. He'd sailed with us through the Caribbean, the Atlantic and the Mediterranean, keeping sharp watch and good company, and bringing us luck. In eight years we'd never suffered a mishap. But during the night of January 2, 1991, that would change.

We were asleep when, just past midnight, our dock lines began to creak. At first I thought a passing boat might have sent a wake, but Santos would have barked. The creaking grew louder. By the time I climbed on deck, the ropes groaned against the cleats that tethered our boat to another vessel.

On such a calm night there could be only one cause—current. My boat was tied stern to stream, and a glance over the side at water speeding past the hull alarmed me. The ebb had tripled its usual spring-tide rate. The cleats on the other boat looked ready to snap. If anything gave, both vessels could spin off bound together, helpless to avoid destruction. I had to cast off.

We were in a difficult spot. Just a few boat-lengths downstream, two high-tension power lines hung across the creek. About 100 feet behind them loomed Denton Bridge. If we couldn't turn in time, our metal mainmast might hit the wires. If the boat hit the bridge, both masts would be pinned by the roadway while the hull was sucked under.

I called everyone up on deck. Sensing something was wrong, Santos stood by, poised to react.

We cast off the lines and hung briefly to a stern anchor, but we had to let go as *Breath* was swung violently back and forth by the current's

force. I gunned the engine and had almost turned the boat around when I realized that, dragged toward the bridge by the current, we were going to hit the power line. Dorothy clutched a quivering Santos, and we all held our breath.

We just tipped the wire. There was a meteor shower of sparks and we were through, but the second wire was coming up fast. I flung the wheel over hard, but we struck the wire anyway—a long, scraping skid, the top six inches of our mast pinned against the power line.

Electricity exploded down the rigging, and a hideous incandescence lit the sky. Flames leapt up inside the cabin; fuses shot from their sockets; smoke billowed out the hatches.

Then the fireworks stopped. The cable had rolled over the mast, but we were trapped between the second wire and the bridge. There was nowhere to go but back out—through the wire. Santos wriggled out of Dorothy's arms and dashed up to the foredeck to be in on the action.

The wheel hard over, we braced for impact. The mast top hit the cable, sending down a torrent of red sparks. Santos, eyes fixed ahead, stood his ground to defend the foredeck. He was growling for all he was worth when sparks landed in his fur. Uttering a high-pitched scream, he sprinted down the side deck, cinders glowing in his coat, and plunged into the water. When he surfaced, Santos was swimming for the boat, his eyes fastened on Dorothy. But the current swept him into the shadows under Denton Bridge and out of sight.

An instant later a blast like a small thunderbolt hit the mainstay. My son Raffy was flipped backward off the foredeck and into the water.

Then we were through. Diego seized a fire extinguisher and attacked the flames as I steered toward a trawler tied to a concrete slab on the muddy bank. Raffy, a college swimmer, managed to get to the bank.

Against all odds we were safe—except for Santos. Raffy called along both shores, but there was no sign of him. We spent the rest of the night tied to the trawler. As I tried to sleep, I kept thinking of Santos. I felt a helpless sorrow over his fate.

The next day Dorothy walked for miles down the beach, making inquiries at every hotel, talking to beach attendants, tourists, vendors. Nobody had seen our little black dog.

She offered a reward over the ship's radio, notified the police and nailed up signs. It was touching, but it seemed futile to me. Just beyond the bridge were broad flats of sand pounded that night by row after row of massive breakers. The thought of Santos funneled helplessly into the surf made me wince.

Days later we'd repaired *Breath,* but Santos still hadn't turned up. "Honey," I told Dorothy, "we've got to get on with our life—do the river, cross the Atlantic, get back to work."

"But what if he survived?" she asked. "What if he finds his way back, and we're gone?"

"It's hard to believe he survived that surf," I said flatly, "and then swam till dawn."

She searched my face, looking for a reprieve from reality. Then her eyes flooded and her voice broke. "I just didn't want to abandon him." With heavy hearts the next morning, we hauled the anchor for our trip upriver.

Our loss really hit home 50 miles upstream where we anchored. Suddenly a strange face peered in the porthole and inquired if we wanted to buy a fish. The fisherman had paddled up silently alongside. When Santos was alive, that could never have happened. Now we sorely missed the zealous barking we'd so often tried to hush.

Not a day went by without someone bringing up another Santos story. He might have been small, but he was absolutely fearless. Santos had a classic Napoleon complex. He had to have respect, and he got it by making bigger animals run from him. He was all bluff. But with a histrionically vicious growl and a headlong charge, he had put to flight Rottweilers, herds of goats, troops of wild donkeys, even a meter reader.

Once, on the island of St. Lucia, an elephant brought over by a rich estate owner emerged from the woods into a clearing where Santos was merrily scattering a flock of chickens. Our dog reacted in character: he charged. The elephant panicked, flaring its ears, splitting the air with its trumpet call and smacking the ground with its trunk as Santos dodged and darted underfoot. We had to catch Santos and drag him away.

We'd never see another like him, I thought as I steered upriver.

Soon after, I woke one night to an empty bed. I found Dorothy sitting in the moonlight. From the way her eyes glistened, I could tell she'd been thinking of Santos. I sat down and put an arm around her. After a while she spoke. "You know what I miss most? His shaggy mane filling the porthole. He liked to watch me cook. Now every time a shadow falls over that port, it reminds me of the love in those bright black eyes."

We watched the moon slip below the treetops; then, our hearts filled with grief, we went back to bed.

Two weeks passed as we made our way 150 miles up the Gambia River. One afternoon Dorothy and I were reinforcing the deck awning when I saw a catamaran with a man on board inspecting us with binoculars.

"Are you the Americans who lost the dog?" he called.

"Yes," I said cautiously.

"I don't know if it is yours, but the police at Denton Bridge have a small black dog found on the beach."

Everyone tumbled up on deck shouting, "Oh, my God! Yes! Yes!" But I cautioned, "Someone might have found a stray mutt and brought it in, hoping for the reward. Don't get your hopes too high."

Dorothy and I took a series of bush taxis and old buses back to Banjul the next morning. With hope and trepidation we caught a taxi to Denton Bridge to see if Santos had truly survived.

"You've come for your dog!" the police officer on duty greeted us. He turned and called to a boy, "Go bring the dog." Dorothy and I waited on tenterhooks.

Then, led on a ratty piece of string down the path, there was Santos. He walked with a limp, head down. But when Dorothy called "Santos," his head shot up, his ears snapped forward, his whole body trembled as that beloved voice registered. He leapt into her arms and covered her face with licks. Dorothy hugged him, her eyes filled with tears.

The police officer told us that the morning after we'd hit the power lines, a Swedish tourist was walking the beach and found Santos—six miles from Oyster Creek. The Swede smuggled the wet, hungry animal into his hotel room and fed him. When the Swede had to fly home, he gave Santos to the police.

Courage is fear holding on a minute longer.

GENERAL GEORGE PATTON

We noticed Santos's muzzle seemed whiter, and when we patted him on his right flank, he sometimes yelped in pain. We wondered what he'd experienced as he was swept into the surf and carried along the coast. We marveled at his fortitude and his luck. But most of all we were grateful to have him back.

Next morning we made our way back upriver. We arrived just after sundown and shouted for the boys.

"Do you have him?" they called. Dorothy urged the dog to bark. His unmistakable voice rang across the river, to be answered by a cheer of wild exuberance.

Later that night we toasted Santos with lemonade. No need for champagne when euphoria spiced the air we breathed. Santos was back. Our family was intact.

LESSON OF THE CLIFF

BY
MORTON HUNT

It was a sweltering July day in Philadelphia—I can feel it still, 57 years later. The five boys I was with had grown tired of playing marbles and were casting about for something different.

"Hey!" said Ned. "We haven't climbed the cliff in a long while."

"Let's go!" someone shouted.

I hesitated. I longed to be brave and active like them, but I'd been sickly most of my eight years and had taken to heart my mother's admonitions not to take chances.

"Come on!" called Jerry, my best friend. "Don't be a sissy."

"I'm *coming!*" I yelled, running after them.

We finally came to a clearing. At the far side loomed the cliff, a near-vertical wall of jutting rocks, earth slides, scraggly bushes and saplings. It was only about 60 feet high, but to me it looked like the very embodiment of the Forbidden and Impossible.

One by one, the other boys scrabbled upward toward a narrow ledge two-thirds of the way to the top. Then, trembling and sweating, I began to climb, my heart thumping in my skinny chest.

At last I reached them, and settled uneasily as far back on the ledge as I could. The others inched close to the edge; the sight made me queasy.

Then they started to the top, from where they would walk home by a roundabout route.

"Hey, wait." I croaked weakly. "I can't—"

"So long! See you in the funny papers," one of them said, and the others laughed.

After they wriggled their way to the top, they peered down at me. "You can stay if you want to," mocked one of the boys. "It's all yours." Jerry looked concerned, but he left with the others.

I looked over the edge and was overcome by dizziness; I could never climb back down. I would lose my grip, fall and die. But the way to the top was even worse—steeper and more treacherous. I heard someone sobbing; I wondered who it was and realized that it was me.

Time passed, and dusk began to gather. Silent now, I lay on my stomach, stupefied by fear and fatigue, unable to move.

January 1945, Watton Air Base, East Anglia, England. This morning I found my name posted on the blackboard: tomorrow I fly a weather-reconnaissance mission in an unarmed twin-engine Mosquito far into German-held territory. All day my mind has whirled. I imagine the shell-burst in the cockpit, the blood and the pain, the fire, the Mossie winging over into a spin while I am too weak to pull myself out of the escape hatch.

Next morning it is clear to me that I can't possibly fly that plane 1000 miles—over the winter sea, into a Europe bristling with Nazi anti-aircraft batteries and fighter planes—and all the way back to safety. I simply can't do it.

January 1957, New York. I'm delirious with joy. I've been offered a book contract by one of the most distinguished American publishers, Alfred Knopf himself.

But later in the day I begin to fear that I have made a terrible mistake. I've suggested a history of love, tracing its evolution from the early Greeks to the present—a vast project, but fun to think about and to sketch in outline form. Yet now that the moment of truth has come, I see how rash I've been.

How could I have imagined I'd ever be able to learn what love meant to the ancient Greeks, to the ascetic early Christians, to the knights and ladies of the Middle Ages, to the—enough! It's impossible, more than I can do.

June 1963, New York. I am lying in bed, sleepless, although it is 2 a.m.; I suspect that my wife, quiet in the dark next to me, is awake too. Tonight we agreed that I should move out as soon as I can.

But I feel as if the ground is giving way beneath me, as if I am falling through space. What will I say to my eight-year-old son? How will my wife and I work out my rights as an absentee father? How can we ever decide how to divide our possessions? I have never lived alone; how will I feel when I close the door at night and am imprisoned in my solitude? No. It is too hard a road to travel. I can't do it.

Twilight, a first star in the sky, the ground below the cliff growing dim. But now in the woods a flashlight beam dances about. I hear the voices of Jerry and my father! My father points the beam upward. "Come on down, Son," he says in a comforting tone. "Dinner's ready."

"I *can't!* " I wail. "I'll fall, I'll die!"

"Listen to me," my father says. "Don't think about how far it is. All you have to think about is taking one little step. You can do that. Look where I'm shining the light. Do you see that rock just below the ledge?"

I inch over. "Yes," I say.

"Good," he says. "Now put your left foot on that rock. Don't worry about what comes next. Trust me."

It seems possible. I gingerly feel for the rock with my left foot and find it. I gain confidence. "That's good," my father calls. "Now, move your right foot a few inches lower to the right and there's another foothold." Again, I do so. My confidence soars. *I can do it,* I think.

One step at a time, I make my way down the cliff. Suddenly I step onto the rocks at the bottom and into my father's strong arms, sobbing a little, and then, surprisingly, feeling a sense of immense accomplishment. It is a lesson I will never forget.

January 1945. I taxi out onto the runway and shove the throttles forward, remembering that all I have to do is take off and climb to 25,000 feet, heading east. Later, the North Sea is just ahead. All I have to do, I tell myself, is stay on this heading for 20 minutes until I cross over Schouwen Island in the Netherlands. I can do it.

Over Schouwen Island, my navigator tells me to turn to a heading of 125 degrees and hold it for ten minutes until we reach our next checkpoint. That's not so hard.

And so it goes. I fly the plane across Holland and Germany, never envisioning the whole trip but only the leg we are flying, until at last we are safely out of enemy territory.

January 1957. After tossing about much of the night, thinking about the impossibly ambitious book I have said I can write, I remember the old lesson once again: I can avoid panic if I look only at the next step.

I'll keep my gaze on the first chapter and read whatever I can find about love among the Greeks; that isn't too hard. Then all I have to do is sort out my notes, dividing the chapter into sections, and write the first part.

Then one exhilarating afternoon two and a half years later, the last of 653 pages emerges from my typewriter and, like a boy, I turn somersaults in sheer joy. Months later, I hold the first copy of my book, and a few weeks after that I read my first major review, praising it.

September 1963. I unlock the door of my tiny apartment, carry my bags in and close the door. I have taken one step of many; it wasn't so hard. The first was to find an apartment. The next was to plan how we'd tell our son about the move, and what each of us would say to reassure him that I'd be nearby and still his father. That, too, proved to be possible. Today, I am moving in; I unpack, make a few phone calls, fix lunch, feel at home.

By the next year, I have constructed a new life. I have acquired the social and emotional skills I need as a middle-aged single man.

I have realized time and again, that, having looked at a far and frightening prospect and been dismayed, I can cope with it after all by remembering the simple lesson I learned long ago on the face of a small cliff. I remind myself to look not at the rocks far below but at the first small step and, having taken it, to take the next one, until I have gotten to where I wanted to be. Then I can look back, amazed and proud, at the distance I have come.

To dare is to lose

one's footing momentarily.

To not dare is to lose oneself.

SOREN KIERKEGAARD

CHRISTOPHER REEVE'S DECISION

BY

CHRISTOPHER REEVE

On Memorial Day weekend, 1995, my world changed forever. I was competing in an equestrian event in Virginia when my horse, Buck, decided to put on the brakes just before the third jump.

When he stopped suddenly, momentum carried me over the top of his head. My hands got entangled in the bridle, and I couldn't get an arm free to break my fall. All six-feet-four-inches and 215 pounds of me landed headfirst. Within seconds I was paralyzed from the neck down and fighting for air like a drowning person.

I woke up five days later in the intensive-care unit at the University of Virginia hospital. Dr. John Jane, head of neurosurgery at the hospital, said I had broken the top two cervical vertebrae and that I was extremely lucky to have survived. He told my wife, Dana, and me that I might never be able to breathe on my own again. But my head was intact, and my brain stem—so close to the site of the injury—appeared unharmed.

Dr. Jane said my skull would have to be reconnected to my spinal column. He wasn't sure if the operation would be successful, or even if I could survive.

Suddenly it dawned on me that I was going to be a huge burden to everybody, that I had ruined my life and everybody else's. *Why not die,* I thought miserably, *and save everyone a lot of trouble?*

As family and friends visited, my spirits were on a roller-coaster ride. I would feel so grateful when someone came a long way to cheer me up. But the time would come when everybody had to leave, and I'd lie there and stare at the wall, stare at the future, stare in disbelief.

When I would finally fall asleep, I'd be whole again, making love to Dana, riding or acting in a play. Then I'd wake up and realize that I could no longer do any of that; I was just taking up space.

One day Dana came into the room and stood beside me. I could not talk because of the ventilator. But as we made eye contact, I mouthed the words, "Maybe we should let me go."

Dana started crying. "I am only going to say this once," she said. "I will support whatever you want to do because this is your life and your decision. But I want you to know that I'll be with you for the long haul, no matter what."

Then she added the words that saved my life: "You're still you. And I love you."

I can't drift away from this, I began to realize. *I don't want to leave.*

A crisis like my accident doesn't change a marriage; it brings out what is truly there. It intensifies but does not transform it. Dana rescued me when I was lying in Virginia with a broken body, but that was really the second time. The first time was the night we met.

It was June 1987, and a long-term relationship of mine had ended. I was determined to be alone and focus on my work. Since childhood I had developed the belief that a few isolated moments of happiness were the best you could hope for in relationships. I didn't want to risk too much because I was certain that disappointment would follow.

Then one night I went to a cabaret with friends, and Dana Morosini stepped onstage. She wore an off-the-shoulder dress and sang "The Music That Makes Me Dance." I went down hook, line and sinker.

Afterward I went backstage and introduced myself. At the time, I was an established film actor. You wouldn't think I'd have a problem with a simple conversation with a woman. But when I offered her a ride to the party we were all going to, she said, "No thanks, I have my own car." All I could say was "Oh." I dragged myself out to my old pickup truck, trying to plan my next move.

Later I tried again. We talked for a solid hour. I have no idea what we talked about. Everything seemed to evaporate around us. I thought to myself, *I don't want to make a mistake and ruin this.*

We started dating in a very old-fashioned way. I got to know Dana's parents, and we developed an easy rapport. And Dana was instantly comfortable with my two children, Matthew and Alexandra. It filled me with joy.

Dana and I were married in April 1992. Three years later came my accident and Dana's words in the hospital room: "You're still you."

I mouthed, "This goes way beyond the marriage vows—'in sickness and in health.'" She said, "I know." I knew then and there that she was going to be with me forever. We had become a family.

As the operation drew closer, I became more frightened, knowing I had only a 50-50 chance of surviving. I lay frozen much of the time, thinking dark thoughts.

My biggest fear had to do with breathing. I couldn't take a single breath on my own, and the ventilator connections didn't always hold. I would lie there at three in the morning in fear of a pop-off, when the hose just comes off the ventilator. After you've missed two breaths, an alarm sounds. You hope someone will come quickly. The feeling of helplessness was hard to take.

One very bleak day the door to my room flew open and in hurried a squat fellow in a surgical gown and glasses, speaking with a Russian accent. He said he was my proctologist and had to examine me immediately.

My first thought was that they must be giving me way too many drugs. But it was my old friend, comedian Robin Williams. For the first time since the accident, I laughed.

My three-year-old, Will, also gave me hope. One day he was on the floor playing when he suddenly looked up and said, "Mommy, Daddy can't move his arms anymore."

"That's right," Dana said. "Daddy can't move his arms."

"And Daddy can't run around anymore," Will continued.

"That's right; he can't."

Then he paused, screwed up his face in concentration and burst out happily, "But he can still smile."

On June 5 I had my operation. It was a success. My doctor predicted that with time I ought to be able to get off the respirator and breathe on my own.

Three weeks later I moved to the Kessler Institute for Rehabilitation in West Orange, N.J. The worst days there were when Bill Carroll, the respiratory therapist, would test my vital capacity, a measure of how much air I could move on my own. I was failing miserably. To even consider weaning yourself off the ventilator, you need a vital capacity of about 750 c.c.'s, but I could hardly move the needle above zero.

At about this time I had to decide if I would attend the annual fund-raising dinner of the Creative Coalition, an organization of people in the arts. The dinner was scheduled for October 16 at the Pierre Hotel in New York City. I felt obligated to go, especially because Robin Williams was to be honored for his charitable work.

Still, I worried about making the trip into Manhattan. It would be the first time I would be in public since my accident in May. Would my muscles go into a spasm as they often did? Would I have a pop-off?

Dana and I talked it over and decided that the psychological advantages of going outweighed the physical risks. We dusted off my tuxedo, and on the afternoon of the 16th, I braced myself for the unknown.

For nearly five months I'd been cruising in a wheelchair at three miles an hour. Now I was strapped in the back of a van driving into the city at 55 miles an hour. As we hit bumps and potholes, my neck froze with tension, and my body was racked with spasms. Once at the hotel, I was quickly transferred to a suite with a hospital bed to rest. The whole experience was more intense than I had anticipated.

At last it was time for me to present Robin with his award. For a split second I wished a genie could make me disappear. As I was pushed onto the stage, though, I looked out to see 700 people on their feet, cheering. The ovation went on for more than five minutes.

From that moment on, the evening was transformed into a celebration of friendship. Later, as we bounced through the Lincoln Tunnel back to New Jersey, I was so excited I hardly noticed the rough ride. Back at Kessler, Dana produced a bottle of chardonnay, and we toasted a milestone in my new life. I'd made it!

I made up my mind—I wanted to breathe on my own again.

On November 2 Bill Carroll, two doctors and a physical therapist brought in the breathing equipment, took me off the ventilator and asked me to take ten breaths.

Lying on my back, I was gasping, my eyes rolling up in my head. With each attempt I was only able to draw in an average of 50 c.c.'s. But at least I had moved the dial.

The next day I told myself over and over that I was going home soon, and imagined my chest as a huge bellows that I could open and close at will. I took the ten breaths, and my average was 450 c.c.'s. *Now we're getting somewhere,* I thought.

The following day my average was 560 c.c.'s. A cheer broke out. "I've never seen progress like that," Carroll said. "You're going to get off this thing."

After that I practiced every day. I went from seven minutes off the ventilator to 12 minutes to 15. Just before I left Kessler, I gave it everything I had and breathed for 30 minutes on my own.

You must do the thing which you think you cannot do.

ELEANOR ROOSEVELT

I'm happy that I decided to keep living, and so are those who are close to me. On Thanksgiving, 1995, I went home to spend the day with my family for the first time since the accident. When I saw our home again, I wept as Dana held me. At the dinner table each of us spoke a few words about what we were thankful for.

Will said simply, "Dad."

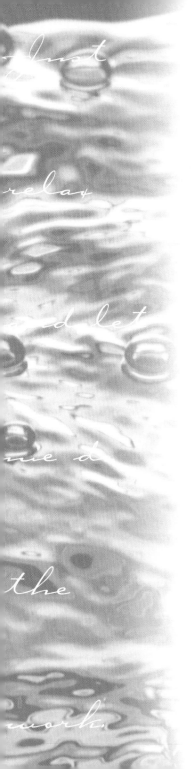

ALONE IN A
SWIRLING SEA

BY

WILLIAM M. HENDRYX

Brutal northeasterly winds ripped through Jim Peterson's Coast Guard warm-up suit as he watched the familiar rescue helicopter lift off from Air Station Elizabeth City, N.C., and disappear into the night. *If only I'd gotten here a few minutes earlier,* the 25-year-old rescue swimmer thought, *I'd be going with them.*

Peterson shook off the cold of this January night in 1995 and went inside to call the maintenance chief. "Something big brewing?" he asked.

"Looks that way," said the chief. "Five guys on a 42-foot sailboat are about 300 miles offshore, and they've been riding this storm for three days in rough seas. The boat's been taking water and is in danger of breaking up."

"Who'd we send?"

"Odom and Vittone," answered the chief. "A C-130 is also en route."

Mike Odom and Mario Vittone were Peterson's close friends. Vittone, 29, a burly, jut-jawed six-footer, had a gruff exterior that hid a soft heart. Odom, a slender 30-year-old, was a quiet sort. The first time Peterson really got to know Odom was when a tornado severely damaged Peterson's house. Odom appeared at his doorstep only hours later, his truck loaded with chain saws and generators. The two men worked two days to clear debris and make the place habitable.

Inside the chopper the co-pilot, wearing night-vision goggles, spotted the circling C-130 and the foundering sailing vessel at 1:20 a.m. Odom and Vittone changed into rubberized dry suits designed to keep a man comfortable for up to 50 minutes in frigid water.

Before boarding the chopper, Odom and Vittone had flipped a coin to see who would go after the first survivor, and Odom had won. "Sorry, Mario!" he said, slapping his friend on the back. "Maybe next time!"

Now Odom hitched himself to the hoist cable overhead and sat in the chopper's open doorway, his legs stretching into the black emptiness, his face stinging from the 45-m.p.h. winds. Looking down, he could see roiling waves cresting at 20 feet and more.

One of the men on the sailboat suddenly tossed a line into the sea and jumped after it. The man grabbed the line with both hands, but a towering wave snatched it from him.

There's no time to lose! Odom thought. He pushed out the door, descended most of the way in the harness, then released it and hit the icy water with a hard splash. In the next instant, he was swallowed in a tumbling wave. Recovering quickly, he swam to the struggling man and locked an arm around his chest. "Just relax and let me do the work," Odom told him.

As the helicopter hovered 50 feet above, Vittone and the flight mechanic tried to move the cable into position to retrieve the survivor. But the powerful winds made the process slow and dangerous. One wrong move, and a rogue wave could swamp the chopper. After several failed attempts, the first survivor was finally hoisted aboard.

Then Odom was lifted from the water, raised through the 100-m.p.h. slaps of the prop wash and pulled aboard. By now the sailboat

had drifted another half-mile downwind. The chopper gave chase, and moments later it was again hovering above the pitching vessel.

Once more, Odom dropped into the water and towed the next survivor—who had also jumped overboard—to the hoist. Each rescue was taking 15 minutes—almost three times longer than normal—because of the darkness and extreme weather conditions. The storm was also taking a toll on the chopper's fuel supply and on Odom.

Back inside the helicopter, Vittone looked Odom squarely in the eye. "Do you want me to take the next one?" he asked.

"I'll do one more," Odom answered wearily. "You can have the last two."

As the third survivor bobbed in the waves, Odom was again lowered from the chopper. Halfway down, however, a 25-foot wave slammed into his body, swinging him wildly from side to side.

His belly full of sea water, Odom hit the surface hard and began throwing up. He'd never hurt more in his life.

Still he swam to the victim and helped him crawl inside the lowered rescue basket. He watched as the man was lifted to safety.

Odom's turn to be hoisted up would come next. He was totally spent and, for a guy who had loved the water since childhood, he'd never been more eager to leave it.

Up above, Vittone could see that Odom was exhausted. Then the co-pilot announced, "Six minutes to bingo," meaning they had just six minutes of fuel remaining before reaching the point of no return. *I wish I'd taken the third survivor,* Vittone said to himself.

While the flight mechanic operated the hydraulic hoist, raising the third survivor, Vittone tried to steady the wild swings of the multistrand steel cable as it glided through his hands. Suddenly he felt a sharp edge

One man with courage makes a majority.

ANDREW JACKSON

cut through his flight glove. *The cable is fraying!* he thought. The high winds had caused it to chafe against the door edge.

"We're losing the cable!" Vittone yelled into his headset. "Run it up!" After several attempts, the survivor was pulled inside the aircraft, but the splintered strands of wire had created a snarled bird's nest inside the hoist housing, jamming it.

Frantically, Vittone and the flight mechanic ran out line, trying to get past the tangle, but it jammed again. They tried a splice, but the winch seized up. Then the co-pilot called out, "Bingo!"

Vittone looked down at Odom, who was signaling urgently for pick-up. *I should stay with Mike,* he thought. But he had to tend to the three survivors in the chopper.

Vittone slumped against the metal wall. Back at the station, there were only two other choppers that could range this far, and both were down for maintenance. It would be hours before this chopper could land and be refueled. Tears welled in his eyes. *It should have been me,* he thought.

Mike Odom watched in stunned disbelief as a bright-yellow life raft and a marker buoy crashed into the water near him. He immediately got the message. "You're not leaving me!" he screamed. With his eyes locked on the hovering craft, he clambered inside the six-man raft. *Maybe,* he thought, *they're going after the sailboat, then coming back for me.* But the chopper spun 180 degrees and flew toward the mainland.

Remembering the radio in his vest pocket, Odom switched it on. "What's happening?" he yelled. The radio crackled, then fell silent. He couldn't get through. Within seconds the chopper's flashing lights disappeared. It was just after 2:15 a.m.

Odom pounded the radio with his fist and collapsed into the raft. *I'm a dead man,* he thought.

Just then, a 30-foot mountain of water hurled the raft through the air and slammed it to the surface, throwing Odom overboard. Quickly he swam to the craft. Grabbing it, he threw his right leg over the two-foot sidewall and rolled onto the floor. Dizzy with nausea, he hung his head over the side, only to be thrown overboard by another wave. *I can't lose the raft,* he thought as he again swam toward it.

Exhausted, still throwing up, he climbed back inside. His face was stinging cold. His hands and legs were losing all feeling. The storm was growing stronger. He felt totally isolated in spite of the C-130 circling above him in the blackness. For a while, the plane's crew talked to him on the radio, trying to boost his morale. But he recognized the cruel reality. A fixed-wing craft could never pluck a man from the open sea.

This is my time, Odom thought. Sitting in waist-deep water, he pulled the 50-foot rescue line from the raft's survival kit and tied it around his body. He leaned against the sidewall and stretched his arms in both directions, lacing them through the webbing of the lifelines in a crucifix-like position. *At least they won't have to spend days searching for my body,* he told himself.

His thoughts turned to Vittone, Peterson and the others back at Air Station Elizabeth City. Unlike Odom, most of them were married with kids. If this had to happen to someone, he figured, it was best that it was to him.

In hopes of rehydrating his water-depleted body, Odom tried drinking the survival-kit water. But he couldn't keep anything down.

Shortly before 5 a.m., he struggled one final time with the small hand-held radio, using his last bit of strength to engage the transmit button. He'd been in the water almost four hours. "I'm cold," he mumbled to the C-130 crew. It was his last transmission.

Aboard the chopper, after failed attempts to contact Odom by radio, the crew focused on survival. The nearest land was 250 miles to the west, and they were flying into 45-m.p.h. head winds. "Give me a fuel calculation!" ordered the pilot.

All eyes were on the co-pilot as he monitored fuel consumption over the next six minutes, then performed some quick calculations. "Looks like we'll have to ditch about 30 miles from shore," he said.

"Run it again!" the pilot ordered.

The co-pilot performed another, more accurate 15-minute fuel-burn count. "We can't make it back to Elizabeth City," he said finally, "but we should make the nearest shore with a pint to spare."

At 4:40 a.m. the chopper landed safely at a small airport in Wilmington, N.C. Vittone called his wife, Kari, who was almost as close to Odom as he was. When she answered the phone, he could hardly say the words. "We had to leave Mike in the ocean," he said solemnly. "I think we killed him."

Jim Peterson had been monitoring the rescue from the Elizabeth City air station. When a second helicopter was pulled out of maintenance to rescue Odom, he was one of the first ones on it. Now, sitting in the rear of the zooming chopper, he glanced out the window. It was just past 6 a.m., and a faint orange glow lapped at the eastern horizon.

Is Mike alive? Peterson wondered. "How much farther?" he asked anxiously.

"We've got a visual on the raft's strobe light," came the reply. "Prepare to deploy."

You'd better be inside that raft, Mike, Peterson thought. He locked his harness to the hoist and sat in the doorway, his legs dangling in the faint light. The frigid wind howled through the hood of his dry suit. The water looked like a boiling caldron. "I'm coming, Mike," he whispered to himself.

The pilot pointed the spotlight directly on the bright-yellow raft. It looked like a tiny toy on the heaving expanse. Peterson's heart pounded. "There's Mike!" he called out. But there was no joy in his words.

The stiff, unmoving body in the raft appeared to be lifeless. The head was down, the arms spread out like the figure of Christ on the cross. There was nothing to indicate Odom was alive.

"Get me down there!" Peterson yelled over the roar of the engines. He swung his body beyond the sliding side door and began a descent. Once in the water, he slid out of the harness and began swimming. He snagged the edge of the raft with both hands and threw his body over the sidewall.

Odom's closed eyes were caked with salt and frost. His body was rigid and icy cold. White foam trickled from his mouth. Peterson grabbed him by the shoulders and shook him hard. "Mike, wake up!" he yelled. There was no response.

He began to massage Odom's chest vigorously, almost pounding it. "Mike, can you hear me?" he yelled.

There was still no movement. In that moment, Peterson could hardly catch his breath as he realized Odom might be dead.

Almost in anger, Peterson grabbed Odom's dry suit and banged his body against the wall of the raft. "Mike! Wake up!" he yelled, tears welling in his eyes.

Still there was no sign of life. Finally Peterson removed his glove to check Odom's pulse. But he couldn't find it.

Just then, Peterson felt something grope at the side of his face mask. He turned to see Odom's left hand reaching out, grasping at him blindly. Peterson cupped both hands around Odom's ashen face and turned it toward him. The crusted eyes were struggling in vain to open. "Come on, pal," Peterson said, fighting his emotions. "Let's get you outta here!"

He pulled the rigid, scarecrow-like figure from the raft and towed him to the hoist line. Then he signaled the flight mechanic to bring them up.

At 6:20 a.m. Mike Odom, cradled in the arms of Jim Peterson, was lifted aboard the chopper. He'd been five hours in the storm-tossed sea. Now he was flown toward the *USS Ticonderoga,* a Navy cruiser that was 120 miles closer than the nearest land-based hospital. In the chopper, he regained consciousness and responded to treatment for hypothermia.

After leaving Odom on the *Ticonderoga,* the chopper caught up with the distressed sailboat. A fourth crewman was taken off, but the storm had abated, and the captain refused to leave his ship. He eventually rode out the storm.

The following day a chopper brought Odom home to a hero's welcome at Air Station Elizabeth City. As he climbed stiffly from the aircraft, there to greet him were his colleagues from the station. Among them were Jim Peterson and Mario Vittone, as well as Kari Vittone. The foursome huddled in a joyful embrace. "I never thought I'd see you guys again," Odom said.

Courage is the art of being the only one who knows you're scared to death.

EARL WILSON

RACHEL REMEMBERS

BY

RICHARD McCORD

A Santa Fe, N.M., teacher received a small book in the mail one day. Its cover was made of blue construction paper. Inside, on pages cut from a looseleaf notebook, were short poems written and neatly illustrated by one of the teacher's former pupils, a little girl I'll call Rachel.

> *School means work*
> *and friends,*
> *quiet hours*
> *sitting at your desk*
> *listening to the rustle of papers.*
> > *That's school.*

When Rachel had entered the teacher's fourth-grade class three years earlier, school had meant none of those things. Partly deaf since early childhood, Rachel wore two strong hearing aids. And the time she had spent in her hushed world when she was younger had left her reclusive and withdrawn. She also stood out because she was tall and thin with red hair, and couldn't catch a ball.

Rachel was bright, however, and early in her life had found refuge in books. In books she had friends. In books she had no handicaps. In books she could do anything.

What if you had your own way
every day?
What would you say?
I'd sail
on a whale
and go to a garage sale.
Listen to an owl
imitate a wolf's howl.
And chase a goon
up to the moon!

During her earlier years in school, Rachel had developed the custom of turning off her hearing aids and sitting quietly in the back of the room reading. When a teacher tried to pull her back into the classroom, she would fly into such a rage that the other kids would stop whatever they were doing and gape at her. And so, more and more, her teachers gave up and left her alone to read.

Rachel's reputation preceded her into the fourth grade at a new school. Both her new teacher and the principal were worried about her effect on the class, and talked of placing her in a class for disruptive children. But Rachel's parents begged the teacher not to give up on their daughter.

So the teacher decided to do her best with Rachel. Whenever the teacher saw her slipping away into books, she made her come back into the lesson at hand. Three or four times a week, flying out of control, Rachel would shout "I won't do this!" and hurl her books off her desk.

But no matter how many times Rachel exploded, the teacher would explain that she was not going to get away with it.

After two months, the outbursts became less frequent, and Rachel slowly began to take part in the class. She started acting like an ordinary student. More than ordinary, for she had read so much that there was hardly a subject to which she could not contribute.

A tree is wisdom.
They stand for centuries.
They know everything.
They quietly watch
and learn and learn.
They will never tell what they know;
                              which is lots.

The other children were still frightened of Rachel. They kept their distance. She had no friends. So the teacher arranged for a demonstration of how a hearing aid works. The kids were fascinated. The teacher asked two little girls who seemed especially understanding to make friends with Rachel. And they did.

Little fish, little fish,
come out of the reeds
on the stream's side,
and play with me.

The rest of Rachel's fourth-grade year got better. The two girls who made friends with her found her to be fun. Soon other children did too. Her enthusiasm for school grew, and when the year drew to a close, the teacher decided to teach fifth grade the next year. She made sure Rachel would be in her class.

That second year Rachel excelled. She had friends. She went on class field trips. Her work in class had few mistakes. But her most wonderful works were her stories.

The unicorn,
so graceful,
leaping across meadows,
playing by starlite,
stopping only
to touch noses
with a woodland creature;
Dawn pierces the sky,
the unicorn goes to
rest upon soft clouds.

Rachel was no longer in the teacher's class in the sixth grade. They would meet on the playground during recess, and it was clear that they both still cared about each other. But Rachel had many other things on her mind: new classes, new friends, perhaps even a boy or two. The teacher understood that Rachel was looking ahead.

In seventh grade, Rachel went off to junior high school. From time to time the teacher called Rachel's parents to ask about her. Cheered by good news, she promised to stay in touch. But her life and work kept her very busy. There were new children whose needs she had to meet.

Then one day, the little book of poems arrived.

A teacher is a friend
who helps you learn math,
English, social studies, science,
reading and fun things.

A teacher is like
another parent,
so caring,
and makes sure
you do your
homework,
and get it right
so you'll have
no trouble as you
grow up,
to maybe
be a teacher
also.

A teacher received a small book in the mail one day. Its cover was made of blue
construction paper. . .

God is my strong salvation;

What foe have I to fear:

In darkness and temptation

My light, my help is near.

JAMES MONTGOMERY

SHE HEARD THE MUSIC

BY

SUZANNE CHAZIN

$\mathscr{S}$he sang almost as soon as she could talk. Standing before a mirror, hairbrush in hand, Denyce Graves would mimic the gospel singers she heard at The Garden of Prayer Pentecostal Church in Washington, D.C. Noting the way music transformed her mother, Dorothy, the little girl decided that it was something you could always call on, even when you possessed nothing else.

To the outside world in the early 1970s, Denyce and her family seemed deprived. Her parents had separated, and her mother, who worked as a laundress and typist, could barely make ends meet. But inside their scrubbed apartment was a secret world filled with the uplifting words of gospel music, encyclopedias and wall hangings reminding the children that hard work and faith were the paths to success.

"You are special," Dorothy told her son and two daughters regularly. "You can do anything."

Sometimes the mother's dreams clashed mightily with reality. On Galveston Street in Southwest Washington, Denyce was ridiculed by neighborhood children for wearing homemade dresses and for her

70

"uncool" taste in music. Bullies mistook her reserve for snobbishness and taunted her for "acting white."

One day, a mentally disturbed neighbor wandered by while the Graves children helped Dorothy wash their car. The woman began cursing at the family, then lunged at them with a broom handle. Dorothy chased the woman away, but when she returned, her hands were shaking. Denyce's stomach churned as she picked up a soapy sponge from the bucket.

Suddenly, from across the car's roof, she heard a deep and gentle hum. Then her mother's rich alto burst forth in a familiar gospel song. Instinctively Denyce joined in. Then the other children followed until their combined voices were as strong as a wall. Singing seemed to make the bad stuff go away.

"There is a public high school that you should consider applying to," Denyce's music teacher, Judith Grove, told her one day in 1977, when Denyce was in junior high school. "It's called the Duke Ellington School of the Arts." Grove handed Denyce an application. "You need an audition to get in."

Grove had first met Denyce in 1974 and was impressed by the nine-year-old child. It wasn't just her clear, strong voice. Grove had heard many equally talented children. In Denyce, Grove saw focus and determination.

Under Grove's tutelage, the tall, gawky girl began to blossom with hope. "I want to perform onstage," she announced to Grove one day. She began singing solos in church and spent extra hours practicing at school. But first she had to escape the streets of her Washington neighborhood. Going to Ellington would be a good start.

Denyce stepped off the bus in Georgetown before a three-story, white-brick high school on a quiet, shaded street of lawns and houses. A young man sat under a tree, playing a trumpet. Another student leaned on a wall, stretching for a dance routine. *This is a school for people who have passions*, she thought. "Please, God," she prayed, "let me pass the audition."

She did, and a few months after Denyce's acceptance, Judith Grove joined her at Ellington after being hired as assistant principal at the school.

One evening, Denyce was invited to a dress rehearsal for Beethoven's opera *Fidelio* at the Kennedy Center. The story behind the 19th-century, German-language opera sounded outdated to Denyce. But as the lights dimmed and the curtains parted, a woman with a voice as smooth as pearls sang of love and anguish, of strength and determination—things Denyce understood.

Later Denyce would tell Grove that the opera was "the most wonderful thing I've ever seen." A few months later, another teacher handed her a recording of "Voi lo sapete," from the opera *Cavalleria Rusticana*. Denyce, mesmerized by the plaintiveness in the woman's voice, played the song over and over until she knew it by heart.

"I want to be an opera singer," Denyce announced to Grove. The teacher saw a brightness, a glow from within. Now music wasn't just an interest or even a passion for Denyce; it was her life.

The teen-ager, however, had no idea what she was up against. Denyce was going to need a formal musical education, and she would soon be competing with kids who'd had years of training. She would have to learn the foreign languages required for studying classical compositions. She'd have to take the private lessons so essential to compete on a world scale.

Then, too, there was the notion, held by some, that black people simply didn't excel in opera. Even Denyce's mother was skeptical.

"But it's what I want to do," Denyce insisted. "I want to travel the world. I want to perform. I want to sing at the Metropolitan Opera House in New York."

Dorothy Graves's heart sank. All these years she had toiled to give her children a better life. And now Denyce, her most studious child, wanted to chuck the security that was within her reach for the highly volatile world of the performing arts.

"If anyone can make this happen, it's Denyce," Grove assured Dorothy. It was time to let go, Dorothy knew. She would have to trust Denyce, and Grove, to navigate a world she couldn't comprehend.

"If you want to be an opera singer that badly, just work hard," Dorothy said finally, "and put your trust in God."

By day, Denyce increased her course load so she could finish school ahead of schedule. By night, she returned to her drab corner of Washington. She knew there was more to the world, and she longed to see it.

In 1981, at 16, Denyce graduated from Duke Ellington and went on to study voice at the Oberlin Conservatory of Music in Ohio. There, she cleaned dormitories, baked doughnuts, delivered pizzas and washed pots to make ends meet. When her voice teacher moved to the New England Conservatory of Music in Boston, Denyce followed.

One day at the conservatory Denyce took part in an opera lab. As she rose to sing an aria from *Werther*, delivered by Charlotte, a woman who marries one man but loves another, students barraged her with questions to get her "in character." "What are you wearing?" "How do you feel?" "What color are you?"

"White," Denyce shot back. The class went silent as Denyce gasped. It was a question she had never considered. *If Charlotte could only be white, then what am I doing pretending to be her? With so few parts in opera that are not defined as white, how can I hope to sing opera at all?*

That night, something clicked inside Denyce. All her life, she had allowed others to label her. She was too white for Galveston Street. She was too black for the opera world. From now on, she decided, she would never let anyone label her again. Charlotte could be anything Denyce wanted her to be, and so could Denyce.

Three years at Oberlin and four years at the New England Conservatory had honed the 23-year-old's voice to a lustrous mezzo-soprano. Denyce was named one of 25 finalists invited to compete for the National Council Auditions of the Metropolitan Opera held in March 1988. It was the moment Denyce had been waiting for all her life. Equally as important as winning the competition was the chance to be noticed and considered for the Met's young-artist training program.

A few months before the finals, however, she began noticing phlegm in her throat and then pain in her vocal cords. "Quit singing before you do any more damage," one doctor advised. She ignored him and went to New York, but had to withdraw from the competition.

She returned to Boston and took a secretarial job. Visits to nearly a dozen specialists failed to pinpoint the problem with her voice.

Denyce even stopped listening to opera. The memories were just too painful. Then late that spring a doctor traced her voice problems to a thyroid condition, correctable with medication. "Now you can sing again," her mother urged.

But Denyce's voice wasn't the only thing that had failed her. For the first time in her life, she'd lost her resolve to continue.

Later that summer, though, the Houston Grand Opera called. Would she be interested in auditioning for their young-artist program? At first she hesitated; the Houston Grand Opera was not the Met.

It's over, she thought. *I can't sing anymore.* Friends and teachers begged her to audition. "We don't stop here," Grove gently admonished her.

There is a time to let things happen and a time to make things happen.

HUGH PRATHER

"God has given you a voice, and you have to use it. Use it in Houston. Use it wherever, but use it."

Denyce went to Houston. The following spring the Grand Opera cast her to play the supporting role of Emilia in *Otello*. The title role went to a guest tenor: Placido Domingo, one of the opera world's most celebrated stars.

To Denyce, this seemed to be the second chance she'd been waiting for. She trained until she was exhausted, only this time her voice grew stronger and more robust. Her old confidence returned. By opening night, she was singing better than ever.

Three years later, in 1992, she received a call. Domingo was scheduled to perform the male title role in *Samson and Delilah* at the Ravinia Festival near Chicago. He had suggested Denyce as his Delilah.

The move to Houston, which had once spelled failure and disappointment to her, had turned out to be the swiftest path to success. Artistic directors were won over by Denyce's heady mix of charm and talent. She was invited to sing in all the great opera houses of Europe and many in the United States. "Graves is, it would seem, a major talent," announced the Los Angeles *Times*. But one dream still eluded Denyce.

It was Saturday, October 7, 1995, and the Metropolitan Opera House in New York was packed. Word had spread that a beautiful 30-year-old American with a full-bodied mezzo-soprano, a magnetic smile and plenty of acting ability was taking the opera world by storm. Playing the lead in Bizet's *Carmen*, about a free-spirited, seductive Spanish gypsy, Denyce Graves had wowed audiences from London to Buenos Aires. And now, after seven long years, the woman who had missed her chance on America's greatest opera stage was making her debut there as its star performer.

Clad in a vampish red-and-black peasant skirt, Denyce Graves strode onstage as if she owned it, fire kindling behind her pantherlike eyes. By the middle of the first act, when, with her hands tied behind her back, she taunted the enthralled Don José, the audience was spellbound.

None of those watching could have been more proud than Dorothy Graves and Judith Grove. They sat staring at the sultry diva with a voice like spun silk. All these years had come down to one moment, one opera, one stage.

At the opera's conclusion, the audience rose for a standing ovation, and as the cheers grew louder, Denyce glowed. If she sang for 50 more years, she knew, this would be the night she would most remember.

Backstage after the performance, Denyce hugged her mother and Grove. When there was nothing before them but a gangly girl with dreams, they both heard the music and saw an artist inside.

Then Denyce turned away to shake hands and sign autographs. When she turned back to catch a glimpse of her mother and teacher, they had melted into the crowd, content to watch from the shadows, knowing that the child who had never lost hope was now living the life she had dreamed.

If you accept the expectations of others, especially negative ones, then you never will change the outcome.

MICHAEL JORDAN

UNFORGETTABLE
BOB BARR

BY

DICK McMICHAEL

$\mathcal{T}$he first time we saw Bob Barr, the 17 members of our band were sitting on the stage at Jordan Vocational High School in Columbus, Ga. We squirmed as he towered above us.

"Let's see how well you can follow me," he said ominously, looking in my direction and lifting his baton. A self-taught drummer, I had volunteered to play our battered bass drum.

At that moment our band was truly the worst in the land. It was 1946, and we were poor kids whose parents worked in mills and foundries. Until a year earlier, we had neither instruments nor a director.

Now, Bob Barr had come to Jordan Vocational to decide if he would take the job. He had distinguished himself as a member of the Indianapolis Symphony Orchestra. But we feared that when he heard us, he would smile politely and walk away.

His baton streaked downward, and we began. It must have sounded terrible. We had inherited junk-store horns and drums. Most of us couldn't read music. But Mr. Barr didn't let on that we played badly.

"Nice!" he whispered to the trumpeter whose first note miraculously hit on cue. "Not bad!" he lied as our last chord echoed in the auditorium.

Then he said to me, "You followed very well!"

It was the first compliment I had ever received. I was a classroom failure. Except for band practice, every school day was torture.

"Will you take the job?" I blurted out as he turned to leave.

He looked at me for the longest time, then said, "I probably will." To this day no one is certain why he did.

Like our families, Robert M. Barr's had little money as he was growing up. When he was five, his father died. His mother worked as a hotel maid in Konawa, Okla. When he was eight, an old Seminole Indian taught him to play trumpet. A local bandmaster coached him on the tuba and got him a scholarship to the Cincinnati Conservatory. There, Bob Barr won a national championship and joined the Indianapolis Symphony. Drafted into the Army in 1943, he was soon directing a soldiers' chorus at Fort Benning, Ga.

"You want to be a real band?" he asked soon after he joined us. We nodded enthusiastically. "Then don't be satisfied until you're the best in the land."

He walked over to a pile of records he had brought and placed one on a turntable. The auditorium reverberated with the majestic fourth movement of Beethoven's Ninth Symphony. We listened in rapt silence. We had never heard such music before.

"Beethoven was deaf when he wrote that," Mr. Barr said at the music's finale. "Are you deaf?"

"No," we answered, wide-eyed.

"Do you have good eyes, strong hands and at least half a brain?"

"Yes!"

"Then," he concluded with a flourish, "you *can* be the best!"

We cheered. For the first time in our lives we let ourselves hope that, maybe, we could amount to something.

Few Jordan students even dreamed of college or good jobs. We expected to take our parents' places in the mills and factories. But Mr. Barr held out a different dream.

"If you want to be the best," he said on our last day of school that year, "it will mean giving it everything you have. Be here for practice tomorrow morning at eight o'clock."

We looked at him, stunned. "Tomorrow is Saturday and Monday we start summer jobs," we said.

"No vacations, no weekends, no summers for us if you want to be winners," he said.

"Yes, sir," we replied. And from that moment we were his.

Bob Barr and his wife, Annie, moved into a red-brick cottage near the school. Often after Saturday-morning practice, Mr. Barr would invite the band home for breakfast. Annie welcomed all with smiles, hugs and endless stacks of pancakes. That little cottage became the band's second home.

One day Mr. Barr said to me, "You're the percussion leader now. The one instrument I can't play is the drum. So you'll have to teach it for me."

It was one of his best tricks: entrust a youngster with responsibilities, then help him accomplish them.

That summer was my happiest. I taught percussion by staying one lesson ahead of my class. When I couldn't figure out a difficult passage, I would knock on Mr. Barr's office door. Together we would talk a little about timpani and cymbals — and a lot about life.

A Bob Barr rehearsal was a never-to-be-forgotten experience. When we reached our goals, he praised us with a smile or a wink. When we failed, he badgered and bullied us. He was known to stop the music, break his baton into little pieces and throw them at an offender.

In two years the band grew from 17 to 85. Mr. Barr personally recruited most of the members. He scrounged up instruments. He visited parents to work out ways to keep every member in the band. He arranged for loans for needy students. Eventually, he persuaded the town to provide us with proper uniforms and a music room.

Mr. Barr loved to plan our half-time shows for Friday-night football. He would walk on the hill above the field and shout orders at us "like Zeus from Mount Olympus," as he put it. He would rush about pinning battery-powered lights to our shoes or stuffing our smallest player into an old bass drum for a surprise appearance at show's end.

In 1948, my senior year, Mr. Barr appointed me drum major. "Next Friday I want you to try something new," he told me. We were out on the practice field. Mr. Barr was dipping a baton into a can of kerosene.

"Twirl it," he said, handing it to me with both ends flaming.

I swallowed hard and began. The flames singed my arms. I tossed the baton high into the air. We both watched the fiery missile falling. It landed, hissing, on the ground.

"Good work, Richard," Mr. Barr said, relighting the baton. "Keep tossing it until you succeed."

Then he added something I have never forgotten: "Whatever you do," he said, "stay with it. See it through. Master it."

During the next six days, I spilled a lot of kerosene and set a patch of field on fire. But on Friday when the lights went out, I tossed that flaming baton high in the air and caught it to thunderous cheers and applause. And I knew what Bob Barr was thinking: *See, you can be the best if you give it everything you have.*

Over time we could hear the difference in our playing. Bob Barr could too. "You must have eaten raw meat and gunpowder for breakfast!" he'd exclaim when we captured the spirit of a great march.

"Get this," he told us after one game. "The coaches sneaked out of the locker room to hear you play!"

Bob Barr wasn't content with traditional band music. Once, as the band sat behind closed curtains before a concert for townspeople, Mr. Barr made a surprise announcement. "Last weekend I told members of the Atlanta Symphony that we would perform the piece by Mendelssohn tonight," he said, grinning wickedly. "They were shocked. They said even if I had successfully worked out an arrangement of the piece for a concert band, high-school players couldn't handle it."

The houselights dimmed. "I bet them you could," Mr. Barr continued, "and they've come tonight to prove me wrong."

Everyone gasped, unable to believe musicians from a symphony orchestra would come to hear the Jordan Vocational High School band.

As the curtains opened, Mr. Barr whispered his usual advice, "Give it everything you got!"

In moments, the band launched into Mr. Barr's arrangement of Mendelssohn. When the piece ended, there was a terrible silence. No one moved. Suddenly, the applause began in waves. People rose to their feet and cheered. Mr. Barr just stood, smiling at his band, tears running down his face. And there, in the balcony, was a scene the band would never forget: members of the Atlanta Symphony standing, waving handkerchiefs and shouting bravos.

Just before my graduation in 1948, Mr. Barr called me to his office. "McMichael," he said, "what do you really want to be?"

"A radio announcer," I said, sharing my secret dream. A few days later, he told me that Ed Snyder at radio station WDAK wanted to see me. Ed soon helped me land my first announcing job and launched my career in radio and television.

Larold Ragland is another of the hundreds whose lives were influenced and careers helped by Bob Barr. Larold, as I recall him, was thin as a rail and looked like he had just fallen off the turnip truck. But Bob Barr saw something in him.

One day Mr. Barr handed him the band's latest acquisition.

"What's this?" Larold said.

"It's a bassoon, and you're going to learn to play it."

Larold gave the instrument everything he had. Before long, he became the first (and only) bassoonist in our band. He went on to become a bassoonist with the National Symphony Orchestra in Washington, D.C.

John Henry Armstrong was failing at school, working nights at the mill, and spending his spare time hanging around a local gym with a gang. Some of its members ended up in prison. Not John Henry. Bob Barr gave him a baritone horn and lessons. Then he scheduled so many practices that John Henry had to drop his gang friends.

When John Henry didn't have $7.50 to buy white shoes to match his uniform, Mr. Barr gave him shoes as a gift. Nevertheless, when John Henry acted up at rehearsal, Mr. Barr tossed him out "forever."

The next day, Mr. Barr stopped practice and yelled, "Where's John Henry?"

"You kicked him out yesterday," I reminded him.

"Well, he's back in today. Go find him."

When John Henry was wounded in Korea, Mr. Barr called his home every day for news. Later, John Henry completed university degrees and today helps handicapped kids.

Because of Bob Barr's example, we achieved in ways we hardly dared imagine. Robert George, whose trumpet skills were honed by Mr. Barr, went on to become chairman of Lummus Industries, the world's largest

Patience and perseverance have a magical effect before which difficulties disappear and obstacles vanish.

JOHN QUINCY ADAMS

manufacturer of cotton gins. Percussionist Jim Fletcher teaches humanities at a local high school — and plays in the Columbus Symphony. And trumpeter Jimmy Cross became chairman of the SouthTrust National Bank in Phoenix City, Ala.

Cross was at New York City's Lewisohn Stadium in 1952 when the Jordan Vocational High School band represented Georgia in the American Legion national competition. The band's concert entry, Beethoven's *Egmont* Overture, moved 50,000 Legionnaires to a standing ovation.

"If we win a prize," Mr. Barr said softly as the band stood at parade rest, "we will not throw our hats in the air. We will be disciplined. We will snap to attention and play our fanfare of thanks."

Already, they had stood for three hours while other bands performed. Legs wobbled, and uniforms were soaked with sweat. A majorette fainted and was carried off. Still, no one moved.

The third-place winner was announced. Its members shouted, hugged and danced. When Mississippi won second place, Southern delegates yelled, screamed and sang a ragged "Dixie."

Then the top award was announced: "The gold cup goes to Jordan Vocational High School."

Two-hundred-twenty heels clicked together, and the audience cheered as the fanfare echoed throughout the stadium.

For that moment, Bob Barr's band was the best in the land. He had planted a dream in our hearts. And in six years the dream had born the sweet, ripe fruit of victory.

After nearly two decades at Jordan, Bob Barr moved east with Annie and their three children to accept a new high-school teaching post. Then, on December 17, 1974, he suffered a stroke that made walking difficult and talking almost impossible. But recognition for his achievements continued. In 1987 the John Philip Sousa Foundation included his Jordan band in its Historic Role of Honor.

On May 17, 1988, Robert M. Barr died in his sleep. He was 69. As the news spread, former band members began seeking a way to pay their respects to the man who had so changed their lives.

A few months later, during a Jordan Vocational High School Friday-night football game, 110 of us from across the nation gathered to play a final fanfare of gratitude.

Middle-aged or older, most of us hadn't prac-  ticed in years. We couldn't fit into the uniforms let alone march the full length of the field. Old instruments had been lifted from dusty cases and polished to perfection. Wrinkled sheets of long buried music, some of it written in Mr. Barr's own loving hand, were taken out and fastened in our lyres.

At halftime, we stood at parade rest. I had volunteered to announce the show on the stadium public-address system: "Ladies and gentlemen, presenting the Bob Barr Memorial Band."

Once again, Jimmy Cross lifted his trumpet. So did John Henry Armstrong, though he couldn't play the first notes. His vision momentarily blurred with tears. Grandmothers and grandfathers marched up the 50-yard line, playing our favorite "St. Louis Blues."

"Give it your best . . ." someone whispered, and suddenly Mr. Barr seemed to be there on that hill, pacing back and forth, yelling orders like Zeus from Mount Olympus: "Play it! Give it everything you've got!" we heard him shout. And we knew that as much as he had loved his music, he loved us more.

Once again we heard the drum major's whistle and played with all our might. The people in the packed stands jumped up, cheering us.

Once again we were marching and playing in Bob Barr's best band in the land.

Courage is the ladder on which
all the other virtues mount.

CLARE BOOTH LUCE

A HEROINE IN HELL

BY

LAWRENCE ELLIOTT

Ⱥ ragged band of children stood in an open area in the Bergen-Belsen concentration camp, shivering in the wind. It was the first week of December 1944, and these few dozen Jewish waifs from Holland, having managed to survive 4½ years of war and many months of imprisonment, were now desperately alone.

They had watched mutely as their fathers and older brothers were loaded aboard a convoy of SS trucks and driven away. No one said where they were going, but some had heard the whispered names of the death camps: Auschwitz, Treblinka, Chelmno.

After the men had disappeared, the trucks came for the mothers and older sisters. After they had been taken away, the children were driven to the women's compound, where they were ordered off the trucks. As the trucks took off, 11-year-old Gerard Lakmaker discovered that his last few belongings, wrapped in a yellow blanket, were gone.

Now huddling together in the black emptiness, the older children tried to comfort the crying babies.

In the darkness of a nearby barrack, a woman named Luba Gercak shook her neighbor awake. "Do you hear that? That child crying?"

"There's nothing," was the reply. "You're having your bad dreams again." Luba clamped her eyes tight, trying to shut away terrible memories.

She had grown up in a *shtetl*, a Jewish community in Poland. Still in her teens, she married a cabinet-maker, Hersch Gercak, and they were blessed with a son, Isaac. They looked forward to more children and a calm life. But then war broke out, and they were sucked into its deadly undertow. Nazis loaded what seemed like all of the region's Jews onto horse-drawn wagons for a nightmare trek to Auschwitz-Birkenau, the most murderous concentration camp in the German system.

As Luba entered its gates, she held Isaac tightly in her arms. But within minutes SS guards tore the three-year-old away. His cries rang in her ears—"Mama! Mama!"—as they threw him up on a truck with others too young or too old to work. Soon the truck rolled away to the gas chamber. Blurred black days followed, and then came the moment she saw a truck dragging the lifeless body of her husband. She felt that she didn't want to live.

But an inner toughness would not let Luba give in. Maybe God had some purpose for her. Her scalp shaven, the number 32967 tattooed on her arm, she talked her way into a job working in the Auschwitz "hospital," a building where the sick were left to die.

Endless days and phantom-filled nights passed. Luba learned German and kept an ear to the ground. One day she heard that nurses were being sent to a camp in Germany. Luba volunteered to go. In December of 1944 she was sent to Bergen-Belsen. There were no gas chambers at this camp, but malnutrition, disease and summary execution made it a gruesomely efficient extermination center.

With the Allied forces closing in and order breaking down, already wretched conditions had worsened. Endless transports

brought ever more starving souls to be jammed into jerry-built, vermin-infested barracks.

Tossing restlessly, Luba again heard the sounds of a crying child. This time, she bounded for the door—then stopped, dumbfounded by the spectacle of a rabble of terrified, shivering children. Luba beckoned them to come closer, and a few cautiously approached her.

"What happened?" she whispered. "Who left you here?"

In halting German, an older boy named Jack Rodri explained that SS guards had brought them there without telling them where they were going. The oldest of the 54 children, Hetty Werkendam, was 14. She was holding Stella Degen, 2 1/2. Others were even younger. Taking Jack by the hand, Luba gestured for the rest to follow.

Some of the women tried to stop her from bringing the children into the barracks. They knew how little it took to provoke the SS, to get a bullet in the back of the head.

But Luba was driven—certain that this was meant to be. She shamed the women by asking, "If these were your children, would you tell me to turn them away? Listen to me; they're somebody's children." And she led the ragged band inside.

In the morning Jack Rodri told Luba their story. Initially, they had been spared the worst of the Nazi atrocities because their fathers made up the backbone of Amsterdam's diamond industry, and the Germans needed their skills in diamond cutting. But the racial fanatics in the Nazi hierarchy finally prevailed. The cutters and their families were sent to Bergen-Belsen. There the parents were eventually taken from the children, who were abandoned where Luba had found them.

Luba's heart soared in gratitude to God for bringing the children to her. He had given meaning to her life again. Her son had been murdered, but she was going to save these children from that fate.

Knowing she could not hide dozens of children, she told an SS officer at the camp what had happened. "Let me take care of them," she said, putting a hand on his arm. "They will never be a problem. I promise."

"You're a nurse—what do you want with this Jewish trash?" he replied.

"Because I am a mother too," she said. "Because I lost my own child in Auschwitz."

Taking this in, the SS officer suddenly realized that her hand was still on his arm. Prisoners did not touch Germans. He struck her full in the face with his fist, knocking her to the ground.

Luba got up, her lip bleeding. But she did not back away. "You're old enough to be a grandfather," she said. "Why do you want to harm innocent children? Babies? They will all die without someone to look after them."

Maybe he was moved. Or maybe he just didn't want to decide what to do with all these children. "Keep them," he muttered. "To hell with them."

But Luba wasn't finished. "They need something to eat. Let me get some bread."

He gave her a note authorizing two loaves. But when she went to the storehouse, three of the boys went with her. Holding her allotted loaves, Luba smiled for the orderly in charge—while the boys stole a few more loaves.

Food became the focus of each day, an unending anxiety. The stipulated ration, one slice of dark bread and half a bowl of thin soup, barely warded off starvation. So every morning Luba set off on her rounds—the storehouse, the kitchen, the bakery—and begged, bartered and stole food. The children crowded to the door when they saw her in the distance. "She's coming! And she has food for us!"

They called her Sister Luba and cherished her as they had their own lost mothers, for it was Luba who scavenged necessities, nursed them when they fell ill and sang lullabies through their long, dark nights. The Dutch-speaking children didn't understand her words. But they understood her love. And in the teeth of all the horrors devised by the Nazis, Luba kept "her children" alive.

Weeks and months marched by. Bergen-Belsen's inmates knew the Allies were closing in. And as the awful winter inched toward the spring of 1945, the Germans tried to dispose of the corpses that littered the camp. But it was a losing battle. Dysentery spread, leaving the children dehydrated, limp with exhaustion, and vulnerable to the raging fever and headaches of typhus.

In a nearby barrack another child from Amsterdam—Anne Frank—succumbed. In their own barracks, a number of Luba's children fell ill. She went from child to child, feeding those who could eat, touching their foreheads with her lips to gauge their temperatures and doling out precious aspirins to the sickest. She prayed for a miracle to save them.

It came on Sunday, April 15, 1945, when a British tank column rolled into Bergen-Belsen. Loudspeakers boomed: "You are free! You are free!" in half a dozen languages.

The Allies brought medicine and doctors, but it was too late for many. There were thousands of corpses lying unburied in the camp, and of the other 60,000 inmates, nearly a quarter died after liberation.

But 52 of Luba's children—all but two of the group she had found 18 weeks before—lived. When they were strong enough to travel, a British military plane took them home. Luba was also on board, looking after them on the way. A Dutch official later wrote: "It is thanks to her that these children survived. As Dutchmen, we owe her much for what she has done."

Temporary shelter was found for the children while they awaited reunion with their mothers, nearly all of whom survived. At the request of the International Red Cross, Luba then accompanied 40 war-orphaned children from numerous other camps to Sweden, where they would begin new lives.

Luba began a new life too. In Sweden she met Sol Frederick, another Holocaust survivor. They married and moved to the United States, where they had two children. But Luba never forgot the others.

Wherever they settled, almost all of Luba's "children" blossomed. Jack Rodri made his way eventually to Los Angeles, where he became a successful businessman. Hetty Werkendam went into real estate in Australia and was voted the country's most successful immigrant. Gerard Lakmaker prospered as a manufacturer.

Stella Degen-Fertig had no recollection of Bergen-Belsen. But as she grew up, her mother told her how much she owed to a woman named Luba; Stella wondered where her protector was.

Others decided to seek Luba. More than five years after being liberated, Jack Rodri managed to talk his way onto TV to tell Luba's story. "If anybody knows where she is," Jack pleaded, "please call this station."

"I do," said a caller from Washington, D.C. "She lives here in the city."

Jack called Luba on the spot. Within the week he was standing in her apartment and holding Luba in his arms. Both wept unashamedly.

Some time later, Gerard Lakmaker, who lived in London, set about organizing a tribute to Luba. The handful who were already in touch began an assiduous search for the others.

On a shining April afternoon in 1995, on the 50th anniversary of their liberation, some 30 men and women—nearly all of whom had last

Be strong and of good courage, do not fear or be in dread of them: for it is the Lord your God who goes with you; he will not fail you or forsake you.

DEUTERONOMY 31

seen one another as children—gathered in the Amsterdam city hall to honor Luba.

His voice charged with emotion, the deputy lord mayor, on behalf of Queen Beatrix, bestowed on Luba the Netherlands' Silver Medal of Honor for Humanitarian Services. Luba was shaken. She didn't know that so many newspaper and television reporters would be at the reunion, or that the deputy lord mayor would make a speech.

After the ceremony Stella Degen-Fertig approached. "I have thought of you all my life," Stella said, struggling to keep her voice steady. "My mother always told me that she had given birth to me, but that I owed my life to a woman named Luba. She said that I was never to forget it." Crying freely, she took Luba into her arms and whispered, "I never will."

Luba clung to her and looked at the others through misty eyes. For this was her real reward: to be with "her children," to know again the love that saved them—and her—from the shadow of the death camps.

Courage is contagious. When a
brave man takes a stand, the spines
of others are stiffened.

BILLY GRAHAM

THE GOOD SAMARITAN
OF WOODBRIDGE

BY

SHARI SMYTH

It was getting close to three o'clock, and Elizabeth "Buddy" Willsher was bustling around the kitchen. Years before, her British-born husband John, a plumber, had taught her how to make a proper tea. Ever since, she looked forward to that hour, sitting next to him at the kitchen table, their arms touching, talking of nothing and everything. The minute she heard John's pickup in the driveway of their home in Woodbridge, Conn., she'd turn on the kettle.

Outside, snow melted under a gritty sky on that Saturday afternoon in February 1995, but in the house smells of baking filled the air. The Willshers' daughter, 18-year-old Jennifer, came into the kitchen and sampled the cake batter with a finger. "I almost forgot," she said. "I have to get Dad a present."

That reminded Buddy of the celebration she'd planned for her husband's birthday. *Next week he'll be 58*, she thought. *Where has the time gone?* John seemed as young and energetic as ever, apart from the painful bursitis in his shoulder. Just that morning as he was getting dressed, it flared up, and she had to help him tuck in his shirt.

John Willsher was heading home on the Merritt Parkway. About a mile from his exit he saw a station wagon barely pulled off the road, leaving little room to be out of harm's way. Willsher swung his truck in front of the car and stopped.

When he walked over to the vehicle, he held up his ID, smiled and said, "I'm John Willsher. I live nearby. Can I give you a lift?"

The woman rolled down her window. "No, thank you, but when you get home, would you please call my husband?"

"Sure will," Willsher said, jotting the number of the back of his hand. He headed back to his truck. He had no intention of waiting till he got home. Once back on the road, he turned off the next exit at a gas station on Whalley Avenue. Across the street there was a 22-foot-wide stream that melting snow had turned into a swollen torrent flowing under a thin shell of ice.

Willsher picked up a phone and called the woman's husband. Just as he hung up, he heard the terrified screams of children.

Then he heard a man yell, "We need a rope." Willsher ran to his truck, grabbed a length of yellow rope and raced across the busy artery, dodging traffic.

Buddy's thoughts drifted back to the first time she met John over 30 years earlier. Mrs. Martin, her matchmaking next-door neighbor, had thought that her boarder, a 27-year-old bachelor, and the striking, blue-eyed Buddy would make a perfect couple. And so, after a little cajoling, here was Buddy at Mrs. Martin's playing the piano. Moments after the piece had ended, Mrs. Martin introduced her to a strapping, sandy-haired man. John Willsher and a friend were headed to a party, but they were late. So after a polite but hurried "Pleased to meet you" from John, the two rushed off.

Buddy strolled home disappointed, thinking, *He's not my type.* That seemed to be the end of it, until one day she and John waved

to each other across their back yards and started talking. They began dating.

Buddy was initially cautious about this man who had come to the United States—almost on a whim—with one suitcase, several hundred dollars and a dream of adventure. He was jovial but had eccentricities. For example, the back seat of John's car was filled with what she thought of as junk: rope, auto parts, duct tape, tools. He considered it all valuable. "You never know when it might come in handy," he'd say cheerily.

He proved it one night when they ran out of gas. He rummaged through his junk until he found a bottle of some kind of fluid, and poured it into his gas tank. That gave him just enough power to make it to the nearest gas station.

And behind his happy-go-lucky exterior, John was much kinder than the other men she knew. There was the time her little brother Dan wanted a motorbike; John helped him build one. The man seemed to be able to build or fix anything. And he had a stubborn notion that he was given this gift in order to help people. More than once Buddy and John were out on a date when he pulled over to help a stranded motorist.

As Willsher scrambled down the bank of the swollen stream, he could see two small boys neck-deep in the icy current. Kerone Smith and Bryan Bates, ages nine and seven, had walked onto ice too thin to support their small bodies. They now bobbed in the water, bare fingers clinging to sheets of broken ice and a tree branch, eyes huge with terror.

On the other side, a man had already crawled out onto the ice. With a bystander holding his ankles, he lay on his stomach and stretched out a tree branch to Kerone. It fell inches short.

Willsher hurled his rope across the stream. The man caught it and tossed one end to Kerone, who grabbed it. Slowly, the man and another bystander pulled the youngster from the water.

The smaller boy, Bryan, screamed, "I can't hold on."

"Yes, you can! I'm coming to get you," Willsher replied. Just a few feet of ice separated him from Bryan. Willsher lay on his stomach and began sliding out to the boy. As Willsher lunged toward the boy, the ice broke, dropping him into the frigid water.

Inches from his hand, Bryan went under. Willsher came up, lunged again, and pulled the boy up by the collar. Now the current pulled him under, but Willsher was able to keep his grip on the boy. Finally Willsher came to the surface, still holding Bryan's face above the icy-cold water.

As Buddy began to prepare dinner, she glanced at the clock. It was past 3 p.m. Whenever John was running late he always called. She reassured herself that he probably had stopped to assist some poor soul in need.

His urge to help, she knew, arose from his childhood. In 1940, when Hitler began his air attacks on England, John was three and living near Colchester, an hour's train ride north-east of London. There were many nights when he listened to the drone of planes and the whine of German bombs ripping into neighboring factory towns. He told Buddy how his parents had to spread thin their meager rations and how they helped their neighbors. Always, he said, the strong helped the weak.

Willsher remembered, too, when his family opened their home to children from bomb-ravaged London. He shared his bedroom with two little boys who cried nearly every night for their parents.

Hearing these stories, Buddy realized what a special man John was, and she knew she was in love. A few months later they were married.

Willsher continued to help others. He was always offering his plumber's skills to the elderly and poor. When a neighbor needed to replace her heating system because it was making her son's severe allergies even worse, Willsher undertook the job, charging only for parts. Word got around. He gained a reputation as the man to call if you needed help of almost any kind. Calls came often, frequently in the middle of the night—some pipes had burst or a furnace had quit. John would say, "No problem, mate," and be off.

He taught their two sons, Michael and Peter, and their daughter, Jennifer, the value of doing good. As soon as they could walk, they'd go along on their father's good Samaritan calls. "In this country we are really blessed," he would tell them, "but we still need to help each other."

Sharing John wasn't always easy, but one night Buddy thought about the difference he had made in hundreds of lives, and how much their children had learned from him. *It's been worth it*, she decided.

But one thing Buddy never got used to was John's casual attitude toward danger. One day shortly after their first child was born, Buddy told John she had heard what sounded like a woman's scream. Grabbing a metal pole from the back of his truck, Willsher ran toward the sound. He saw two men locked in a brutal fight.

Outraged, Willsher sprinted toward the attacker, pointing the pole at him like a javelin. "Stop it!" he yelled. The thug jumped into his station wagon and drove straight at him. For a few chilling seconds Willsher stood his ground and, with all his strength, hurled the pole at the car, smashing it through the windshield. The driver swerved and sped off. Later, police caught the man with the distinctive hole in the windshield.

But Buddy was horrified at John's recklessness. "I can't stand by and do nothing," he replied.

Seeing Willsher foundering in the water, a man on the far shore scooped up the rope and flung it to a bystander on Willsher's side. When Willsher surfaced, the man threw him the rope. With his free hand he grabbed it, and with the other, he clutched the boy. The two were dragged to shore. Willsher slumped to the ground, exhausted from the ordeal. Several people scooped Bryan up and rushed him away.

By now a crowd had gathered. A cheer went up when they realized both boys were saved. Amid the congratulations, one onlooker, a physician's assistant, glanced across the river. He noticed Willsher lying face down. "Check that man," he yelled.

Buddy looked at the kitchen clock for what seemed like the hundredth time, as if that would bring him home. Then the ring of the phone interrupted her thoughts. It was the hospital.

Racing there in her car, Buddy clung to the hope that John's iron will would save him. "Please, God," she begged, memories surging.

A hospital staffer met Buddy at the emergency room.

"I'm sorry," was all he could say.

The strangest, most generous, and proudest of all virtues is true courage.

MICHEL DE MONTAIGNE

John Willsher was buried three days later on February 14, 1995. The service was packed with relatives, friends and strangers who had read about the heroic good Samaritan in the local paper. Even the governor of Connecticut was there. Buddy's brother, for whom Willsher had built the motorbike so many years before, gave one of the heartfelt tributes:

"There were two gifts given on Saturday: the first, the gift of life, John gave to Bryan Bates. The second was God's gift to John, eternal life. John is here in our minds, where we'll always think of him; he's here on our lips, where we'll always speak highly of him; he's here in our hearts, where we'll always love him."

Willsher's daughter, Jennifer, concluded the ceremony with her own tribute. "When we think about Dad, the one word we think of is 'hero.'"

MR. LEE'S SIDE OF THE STREET

BY

KREGG SPIVEY

When Hattie Robinson moved from a lonely farm outside Tallahassee to West Perrine, Fla., this suburb of Miami was a friendly neighborhood of small frame houses. Neighbors visited one another in the evenings, and the children played tag in the shadows of the street lights. People went to sleep with their screen doors unlatched. It was a good place to raise her grandson, Lee Arthur Lawrence, whose mother and father had split up.

Lee loved West Perrine, but Hattie's income as a domestic was small and her frail health often kept her from working at all. When it looked as if they'd have to return to the farm, Lee quit school for a dollar-an-hour job at a sewing-machine company. Though Hattie remained sickly, Lee's paycheck got them by through the years.

When he was 24, Lee met Sarah Hagins at a church choir concert. Two years later they were married and in time had two children, Nita and Junior. Sarah was a teacher's aide; Lee worked at a convenience store. Hundreds of people came by during the day to pick up bread and milk. Kids stopped for snacks, and Lee talked to them all, keeping his finger on the pulse of the neighborhood.

Lee and Sarah saved enough for a down payment on a house. Two years later a building became available for rent on 104th Avenue. Lee told Sarah he wanted his own store. They withdrew all their remaining savings, two thousand dollars, and opened "Lee's Grocery."

Lee's business prospered, but his beloved West Perrine was changing. Men and women were hanging out on street corners. There were craps games, fights. Drugs were being sold. People no longer felt safe visiting their neighbors after dark.

Yet in Lee's mind, the neighborhood of his youth was still here; it just needed a little sprucing up. "This is our home," he told Sarah. "If I had a million dollars, I wouldn't live anywhere else."

Lee joined civic groups: Optimists, Jaycees, parent-teacher associations. And he got involved with the kids who came to his store.

"Getting in trouble in school, eh?" Lee looked across the counter at a 12-year-old named Derrick, who waited to pay for his potato chips and chocolate drink. Derrick's father had been lost in a mission over Hanoi in 1972, and the boy had only his mother to raise him. "Can't get along with the teacher?"

"Hate her!"

"Well, what you going to do for a job if you get kicked out of school?"

"When I get old enough, I'll go with the pros," Derrick answered confidently.

"I quit school." Lee gave him a solemn look. "That was the end of my football career. If I had stayed in school, gone on to college, I'd be playing for the Dolphins today — quarterback!"

Derrick's mouth dropped open. He looked at Lee with wide eyes, believing every word. "Ooooh, Mr. Lee!" he said pityingly. Then he walked slowly to the door. From the corner of his eye, Lee watched Derrick head toward school with the other kids.

Lee loved the kids. He'd banter with them in the mornings before school. "Hi, Evan. Hi, Junior. What can I do for you gentlemen this morning? Cookies and milk, okay. Crackers and soda, okay. Three candy bars! You don't need three candy bars!" Sometimes, he'd slip something extra into the bag of a child he knew didn't get enough for breakfast.

Lee watched the kids as they walked across the parking lot. They stayed on the west side — his side — of the street. He advised them not to walk on the other side where the junkies congregated.

Lee realized that the kids of West Perrine needed something to build character and discipline, something to foster teamwork. He decided to sponsor a team in the Optimist football program.

Soon Sarah was picking up the Richmond-Perrine Optimist Club "Giants" with the van after school, driving team members two miles to Richmond Heights Park and then returning to the store to help Lee. At 7:30, Lee brought the players home.

Lee became a familiar presence at the three neighborhood schools. He'd show up to bring back a truant or a suspension case. He'd get parents, teachers and administrators together to renegotiate an expulsion. Didn't they know there were drugs out on the street?

If Lee couldn't get a parent to come to a child's aid, he'd vouch for the kid himself and guarantee good behavior.

During the 1980s, a new drug called crack began to flood the streets. It seemed to take possession of those who smoked it, with a vicious, hungry addiction.

Like zombies, the crack heads rummaged for food and aluminum in the parking-lot trash cans of Cutler Ridge and Quail Roost malls late at night. They used shopping carts to trundle their found and stolen metal to the recycling center on 184th Street.

Businessmen up and down U.S. Route 1 packed up and left. Lee watched families put locks and bars on doors and windows, barbed wire around yards. But he kept the old neighborhood locked away like a treasure in his mind. He could help bring it back; he was sure of that. So he opened a larger grocery next to the old one. Hattie, though 83 and very ill, rolled down the shining aisles in her wheelchair, swelling with pride.

When Hattie died a few weeks later, Lee took stock. If God had put Hattie on earth for the purpose of raising him, then surely God had a purpose for him too. Lee tacked up a sign on the wall behind the counter of his new store:

Lord, help me to remember
That nothing is going to happen today
You and I can't handle together.

When drug dealers tried to set up shop in his parking lot, he'd walk up to them and say, "Please, I don't allow that on my property."

Lee's store became a drug-free island in a sea of crack and cocaine, a haven for the neighborhood kids who came to the store to get their before- and after-school snacks.

"Look here, y'all," Lee would tell them, "I don't care how big you gettin'. Y'all stay on *this* side of the street."

"Yes, sir, Mr. Lee," they would chorus, and when they left they walked on Mr. Lee's side of the street — because they knew he was watching.

When a family opened a restaurant and store next door in the building Lee had vacated, the drug trade gravitated to it. Lee kept an eye on the dealers frequenting the place. He called the cops whenever there was a disturbance. The dealers knew that they had an enemy. But Lee never gave that a thought. He was working for a better community.

Lee threw himself into more neighborhood organizations. He joined the Community Action Agency, the Perrine Crime Prevention

Courage is the resistance to fear, mastery of fear, not absence of fear.

MARK TWAIN

Center Advisory Board, the West Perrine Community Development Corporation.

"Are you coming to the meeting?" became Lee's standard greeting for customers entering his store. Most would pacify him with a "yes" but seldom followed through by showing up. Lee wanted to talk about increasing police patrols and getting dealers off the streets. But it seemed that few of his neighbors cared enough to help. Some were intimidated and feared for their lives if they were to speak out.

Lee, Sarah, Nita and Junior worked shoulder to shoulder at the store. On Friday nights they went to high-school football games to watch Derrick and Junior play, and on Sundays, they sat in the Orange Bowl, rooting for the Dolphins.

West Perrine continued to deteriorate. More and more businesses closed, their owners tired of working behind concertina wire, intimidated by holdups and shootings. But Lee refused to give up. He continued to work with kids. He continued calling the cops and fingering pushers.

A few days before Christmas in 1986, Lee pulled into his driveway and got out of the car. Suddenly, a popping sound drew his attention to the lot across the street. A man stood there, arm extended, firing a pistol at him. By the time Lee understood what was going on, the gunman had fled. Another night, just as he entered the house, there was the sharp blasting noise of a burglar alarm from around the corner. The store!

The family found the front window shattered. A pint wine bottle filled with gasoline and stoppered with a charred rag lay on its side on the counter. Gasoline was dripping onto the floor. They found another Molotov cocktail — still intact — under the potato-chip rack.

These attacks only made Lee more determined. He went into the schools and told the kids about the dangers lurking on the streets. He told them how easy it was to get into trouble and how hard it was to get out.

Soon, the press began to hear about this tireless community worker who couldn't be intimidated. "I don't profess to be important or anything like that," Lee told one interviewer. "If more people would stand up to the dealers, we wouldn't have these problems."

Although police had stepped up their patrols of Lee's neighborhood, he was assaulted again a few months later, as he got out of his car. Nita, in bed under a front window, heard a gun being cocked. "Daddy, get down!"

The chink and whiz of bullets striking the brick and stone of the house filled the night. Bullets thudded into the heavy wooden door and into the sheet metal of the car and the van. Finally the night was quiet except for Nita's high-pitched sobbing. "You've killed my father!"

Sarah crept from the hall to the living-room window to see if her husband was all right.

There was the sound of crickets, then a hushed, "Open the door."

Lee rushed in from his sanctuary behind the car. Sarah threw her arms around him. "You've got to stop now. It's time to let somebody else do something."

Lee held her by the shoulders and said, "That attitude is what's wrong with West Perrine."

No arrests were made.

Shortly afterward Lee told Sarah about a vision. "Can you imagine," he said," *all* the churches in the neighborhood marching together? Can you see the churches giving up a morning to march up Homestead Avenue to let the drug pushers know we won't take it anymore?"

Sarah stood transfixed. "Would they do that?"

"They've got to," Lee answered. "We're going to lose this neighborhood unless we can get these churches together."

One March evening last year, as Lee went about his usual closing routine, a young man sat on a bicycle outside the store, his pet bulldog at his side. Lee came out to pick up trash in the parking lot. At that moment, a man wearing camouflage clothing stepped around the corner. He pulled out a semi-automatic weapon and began firing.

The dog took the first hit. Then the young man on the bicycle fell, critically wounded in the spray of bullets. Lee turned to face the gunman, and a bullet knocked him down. Another man emerged from the store and began shooting Lee as he lay motionless on the pavement. When it was over, the man everyone called "Mr. Lee" lay in the litter-strewn parking lot. He was dead, 12 days from his 52nd birthday.

The world is before you, and you need not take it or leave as it was when you came in.

JAMES BALDWIN

More than a thousand people tried to crowd into the funeral services at Mt. Sinai Baptist Church, a building that was meant to hold hundreds. Condolences came from all over the nation, from servicemen abroad, from kids who had grown up in West Perrine. Miami developer Jeb Bush read a letter from his father, the President. "It takes a special man to stand up for what he believes," Bush read. "He will be remembered with great respect."

Derrick Thomas, voted the nation's outstanding college linebacker, drove 12 straight hours from the University of Alabama through a rain of tears. "I know Mr. Lee is up there with my dad, looking down," he said. "If I could say one thing to him now, I'd say, 'Look, Mr. Lee, I'm walking on your side of the street.' "

Police charged four men with murder. Sweeps of the neighborhood led to hundreds of drug arrests. Newspaper and television reporters flocked to West Perrine. They called Lee a martyr in the war against drugs. But the question remains: why did Lee do it? He did it because West Perrine was his home, *his* neighborhood. "As the saying goes, it's better to light one candle than to curse the darkness," says Sarah. "He wanted to light a candle."

Church bells decorated the air of West Perrine the Sunday after Lee's funeral. Sarah, Nita and Junior gathered at the park near Lee's store and began to walk through the neighborhood. They linked arms and marched up Homestead Avenue, their voices ringing out in every corner of the neighborhood, "We shall overcome; drugs and crime must go!"

A ragged figure pushing a shopping cart filled with aluminum cans stopped and listened. From behind torn curtains and battered doors, pushers and junkies looked out in amazement at Lee's family . . . and the 3000 men, women and children behind them — the extended family of churches — who had come to clap and sing and make Lee's dream come true.

THE RUSSIAN WHO NEVER FORGOT

BY
CHARLES KURALT

In May 1988, I was in Moscow helping out with coverage of the Reagan-Gorbachev summit meeting. The hotel where I was staying, the gigantic Rossiya, which looms behind Red Square, was closed to Soviet citizens that week. All comings and goings were regulated by grim-faced KGB men.

We American and Western European reporters wore credentials on chains around our necks to get into the building past the guards. Dr. Asseyev got in on his medals.

He wore his World War II medals on the lapels of his suit coat, as do many old soldiers in the Soviet Union. When the KGB stopped him at the front door of the Rossiya, the old man erupted in indignation.

"What do you mean I cannot enter? You pups! You have the gall to tell a veteran of the Great Patriotic War he cannot pass into a common hotel lobby?"

He slapped the place over his heart where his medals hung. When the young chief of the guard detail came over to see what the shouting

110

was about, the old man demanded, "Where were YOU when I received these honors?" His voice rose even louder as he answered his own question. "On your mother's lap?"

The chief started to speak, but the old man interrupted him. "Where were YOU when the Gestapo gave me THIS?" he shouted, pointing to a deep scar over his right eye. He then jutted out his square chin and paused for a reply.

The KGB man shrugged and, without a word, stood aside.

Minutes later, the chunky character ranting in Russian showed up in the CBS news offices, insisting that he be heard. A young Russian-speaking assistant took the old man into a vacant room, listened to him for a few minutes and sent him home — but only after promising that a CBS News reporter would see him the next day.

And that is how it happened that the next morning I went for a walk in a park with Dr. Nikita Zakaravich Asseyev.

He wore his medals. He carried his walking stick in one hand and a worn shopping bag in the other. We were accompanied by an interpreter, but Dr. Asseyev kept forgetting to wait for his words to be translated. He was in a great rush to say what he had to say.

"You have to help me. You are my hope," he said. He shifted his cane to the hand that held the shopping bag and grasped my arm. "You can speak to America, is this not true?" he asked. "You must help me find some Americans I knew during the war. I have to thank them for saving my life and the lives of many Russian soldiers."

We sat down on a park bench. He cleared his throat and began.

"We were all prisoners of the Germans at a big concentration camp at Fiiurstenberg on the Oder River. There were about 3000 American soldiers there.

"The camp was laid out this way." With his cane, he drew a map on the ground. "Here the town, here the river and the railroad tracks, here

the camp, Stalag III-B. Here the French prisoners, the Polish, the Yugoslav." For each, he drew a large rectangle.

"Here," he said, drawing the largest enclosure of all, "the Russians. And next to us, just across the wire fence — the Americans. At least 25,000 men died in that concentration camp."

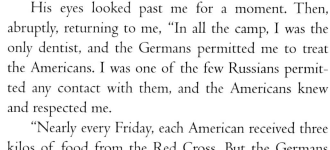

His eyes looked past me for a moment. Then, abruptly, returning to me, "In all the camp, I was the only dentist, and the Germans permitted me to treat the Americans. I was one of the few Russians permitted any contact with them, and the Americans knew and respected me.

"Nearly every Friday, each American received three kilos of food from the Red Cross. But the Germans gave us only one liter of turnip soup and one liter of water per day. It wasn't enough to keep us alive. We were dying by the tens, and then by the hundreds. The Americans could see this.

"One day, after I had been there about a year, two American brothers named Wowczuk, Michael and Peter, and a third American whose name I forget, proposed a plot to smuggle food to the Russians."

"Wasn't that dangerous?" I asked.

Dr. Asseyev threw up his hands. "Of course!" he exclaimed. "Many men were executed for much less!"

"How did the Americans get the food to you?"

The old man smiled. "They waited until the sentry had passed at night and threw the parcels over the ten-foot fence," he said. "I organized a group on our side to rush out and retrieve the packages. One month we received about 1300 parcels."

Dr. Asseyev took my arm again and gripped it tightly. "Do you realize what I am saying?" he asked me. "This was over 9000 pounds of food! Do you know what this food meant on our side of the wire, where men were dying every night of starvation?"

He released my arm. "This went on," he said, "for months. Many Americans risked their lives to dash out at night to throw food parcels to us. Not one ever failed to make it across the wire."

"Why do you think the Americans did this?" I asked.

"Because we were allies," Dr. Asseyev answered. "And because they were good men.

"But now I want to tell you about the behavior of the Americans when the plot was discovered. Late in May 1944, all 3000 American prisoners were assembled on the parade ground. It was a hot day. Four SS officers went down the line, saying to each one, 'Give us the name of the Russian who organized this plot.'

"For three hours in the sun, with nothing to drink, the Americans stood there with clenched lips. The German officers threatened them with severe reprisal. But not one American gave my name.

"Finally, to bring the thing to an end, the brothers Wowczuk stepped forward. 'The whole thing was our idea,' they said. German guards seized them, and the brothers were driven out of the camp. Later I learned they were taken to a camp where they were questioned every day for four months by the Gestapo. I was afraid for them, but I had no fear for myself. I knew that Michael and Peter would never reveal my name. And they did not."

Dr. Asseyev smiled and lowered his voice. "Later we were all moved to a different camp," he said, "and do you know — I found Michael and Peter there. And within a few days, we had organized the plot all over again!"

He beamed triumphantly and started rummaging around in his shopping bag. "After the war," he said, "I wrote down the names of those Americans so I would never forget them." He showed me a carbon copy of a document of seven pages, typed in Cyrillic characters. It was dated September 1, 1949.

"This is for you," he said. "It tells the names of the Americans and what I remember about them. For now, I will tell you the names only."

Gravely, he began to read. "Wowczuk, Michael . . . Wowczuk, Peter . . . Jarema, William. He was from New York . . . Harold Simmons. He was from Kalamazoo, Mich. . . . Walhaug, Lloyd. He was a farmer from Minnesota . . . Gasprich. How I loved Gasprich!"

He looked up from the paper. "What good men they all were!" He took out a handkerchief and wiped his eyes. Then he continued reading: "Brockman. Doctor. Captain. I will tell you more about Brockman . . . Dr. Hughes. He was a good friend. . . ."

I sat on a park bench listening to these American names pronounced in a Russian accent. I knew I was hearing a roll call of heroes.

He leaned forward and said to me, "Four of us Russian doctors in the camp took an oath after the war that we would find a way to thank these Americans. I am getting old now. This is my chance.

"Because of you," he said, "if these men are still alive they will know I remember — this dentist who loved them, and whom they did not betray."

He stopped. He exhaled deeply, handed me the list of names and slumped back on the bench. After 43 years Nikita Zakaravich Asseyev had just fulfilled an oath.

I invited him to lunch. At the table, Dr. Asseyev produced more keepsakes from his shopping bag. There were photographs of the abandoned camp and of the Russian doctors who had survived Stalag III-B with him. Finally there was a crude cigarette case made of hammered tin.

"Late in the war," said Dr. Asseyev, "Dr. Brockman, with whom I had many long and searching conversations, left the camp. Before he left, he gave me this."

Into the top of the case was scratched the inscription, "To N. S. Asseyev from Sidney Brockman, Captain, U.S. Army."

After lunch I walked Dr. Asseyev to the taxi that would take him home. "I know you will not fail me," he said.

The next morning I left Moscow for London with the videotape cassettes of Dr. Asseyev's story. In London, they were edited for that night's "Evening News." And once more, on tape, Dr. Asseyev recalled the names.

"Wowczuk . . . Simmons . . . Jarema . . . Brockman . . ."

"Listen to these names back there in America," I said. "If your name is on this list, an old soldier is saying thank you."

Watching the news that night, Dr. Sidney Brockman, retired from the San Antonio Health Department, felt tears spring to his eyes. "We were all very close to Dr. Asseyev," he explained later. "We all had tremendous respect for the man, because we knew the Russian prisoners were having things mighty rough.

"When Russian prisoners died in their barracks in the winter, their comrades did not report their death to the Germans. They stood them up for roll call so the bodies would be counted for rations."

He took out a handkerchief and dabbed at his eyes. "How could we not try to help them?" he asked. He paused to collect himself. "I have not forgotten Dr. Asseyev. I will never forget him."

He got up, went to a cedar chest and after a time found what he was looking for. "I took it with me when I left the camp," he said. "It's about the only thing I've kept from the war."

It was a handmade cigarette case fashioned out of scrap wood. He opened the case and shook a small metal plaque into his hand. The plaque read, "Sidney Brockman from N. S. Asseyev."

I did my best to deliver Dr. Asseyev's message of gratitude to all those on his list. Some have died, among them the brave brothers Wowczuk. One or two find the memory of Stalag III-B so painful that even now they refuse to discuss it.

"To see what is right and not do it, is want of courage."

CONFUCIUS

By a recent act of Congress, World War II prisoners-of-war have been awarded decorations years after their imprisonment. None of the heroes of Stalag III-B ever have been honored for what they did there — except in the memory of an aging Russian dentist.

Courage is not limited to the battlefield or the
Indianapolis 500 or bravely catching a thief in
your house. The real tests of courage are much
deeper and much quieter. They are the inner tests,
like remaining faithful when nobody's looking, like
enduring pain when the room is empty,
like standing alone when you're misunderstood.

CHARLES R. SWINDOLL

TWO WORDS TO AVOID,
TWO TO REMEMBER

BY

ARTHUR GORDON

$\mathcal{N}$othing in life is more exciting and rewarding than the sudden flash of insight that leaves you a changed person — not only changed, but changed for the better. Such moments are rare, certainly, but they come to all of us. Sometimes from a book, a sermon, a line of poetry. Sometimes from a friend . . . .

That wintry afternoon in Manhattan, waiting in the little French restaurant, I was feeling frustrated and depressed. Because of several miscalculations on my part, a project of considerable importance in my life had fallen through. Even the prospect of seeing a dear friend (the Old Man, as I privately and affectionately thought of him) failed to cheer me as it usually did. I sat there frowning at the checkered table-cloth, chewing the bitter cud of hindsight.

He came across the street, finally, muffled in his ancient overcoat, shapeless felt hat pulled down over his bald head, looking more like an energetic gnome than an eminent psychiatrist. His office was nearby; I knew he had just left his last patient of the day. He was close to 80, but he still carried a full case load, still acted as director of a large foundation, still loved to escape to the golf course whenever he could.

By the time he came over and sat beside me, the waiter had brought his invariable bottle of ale. I had not seen him for several months, but he seemed as indestructible as ever. "Well, young man," he said without preliminary, "what's troubling you?"

I had long since ceased to be surprised at his perceptiveness. So I proceeded to tell him, at some length, just what was bothering me. With a kind of melancholy pride, I tried to be very honest, I blamed no one else for my disappointment, only myself. I analyzed the whole thing, all the bad judgements, the false moves. I went on for perhaps 15 minutes, while the Old Man sipped his ale in silence.

When I finished, he put down his glass. "Come on," he said. "Let's go back to my office."

"Your office? Did you forget something?"

"No," he said mildly. "I want your reaction to something. That's all."

A chill rain was beginning to fall outside, but his office was warm and comfortable and familiar: book-lined walls, long leather couch, signed photograph of Sigmund Freud, tape recorder by the window. His secretary had gone home. We were alone.

The Old Man took a tape from a flat cardboard box and fitted it onto the machine. "On this tape," he said, "are three short recordings made by three persons who came to me for help. They are not identified, of course. I want you to listen to the recordings and see if you can pick out the two-word phrase that is the common denominator in all three cases." He smiled. "Don't look so puzzled. I have my reasons."

What the owners of the voices on the tape had in common, it seemed to me, was unhappiness. The man who spoke first evidently had suffered some kind of business loss or failure; he berated himself for not having worked harder, for not having looked ahead. The woman who spoke next had never married because of a sense of obligation to her widowed mother; she recalled bitterly all the marital chances she had let go by. The third voice belonged to a mother whose teen-age son was in trouble with the police; she blamed herself endlessly.

The Old Man switched off the machine and leaned back in his chair. "Six times in those recordings a phrase is used that's full of a subtle poison. Did you spot it? No? Well, perhaps that's because you used it three times yourself down in the restaurant a little while ago." He picked up the box that had held the tape and tossed it over to me. "There they are, right on the label. The two saddest words in any language."

I looked down. Printed neatly in red ink were the words: *If only.*

"You'd be amazed," said the Old Man, "if you knew how many thousands of times I've sat in this chair and listened to the woeful sentences beginning with those two words. 'If only,' they say to me, 'I had done it differently—or not done it at all. If only I hadn't lost my temper, said that cruel thing, made that dishonest move, told that foolish lie. If only I had been wiser, or more unselfish, or more self-controlled.' They go on and on until I stop them. Sometimes I make them listen to the recordings you just heard. 'If only,' I say to them, 'you'd stop saying *if only,* we might begin to get somewhere!' "

The Old Man stretched out his legs. "The trouble with 'if only,'" he said, "is that it doesn't change anything. It keeps the person facing the wrong way—backward instead of forward. It wastes time. In the end, if you let it become a habit, it can become a real roadblock, an excuse for not trying anymore.

"Now take your own case: your plans didn't work out. Why? Because you made certain mistakes. Well, that's all right: everyone makes mistakes. Mistakes are what we learn from. But when you were telling me about them, lamenting this, regretting that, you weren't really learning from them."

"How do you know?" I said, a bit defensively.

"Because," said the Old Man, "you never got out of the past tense. Not once did you mention the future. And in a way—be honest, now! —you were enjoying it. There's a perverse streak in all of us that makes us like to hash over old mistakes. After all, when you relate the story of some disaster or disappointment that has happened to you, you're still the chief character, still in the center of the stage."

I shook my head ruefully. "Well, what's the remedy?"

"Shift the focus," said the Old Man promptly. "Change the key words and substitute a phrase that supplies lift instead of creating drag."

"Do you have such a phrase to recommend?"

"Certainly. Strike out the words 'if only'; substitute the phrase 'next time.' "

"Next time?"

"That's right. I've seen it work minor miracles right here in this room. As long as a patient keeps saying 'if only' to me, he's in trouble. But when he looks me in the eye and says 'next time,' I know he's on his way to overcoming his problem. It means he has decided to apply the lessons he has learned from his experience, however grim or painful it may have been. It means he's going to push aside the roadblock of regret, move forward, take action, resume living. Try it yourself. You'll see."

My old friend stopped speaking. Outside, I could hear the rain whispering against the windowpane. I tried sliding one phrase out of my mind and replacing it with the other. It was fanciful, of course, but I could hear the new words lock into place with an audible click.

"One last thing," the Old Man said. "Apply this little trick to things that can still be remedied." From the bookcase behind him he pulled out something that looked like a diary. "Here's a journal kept a generation ago by a woman who was a school-teacher in my hometown. Her husband was a kind of amiable ne'er-do-well, charming but totally inadequate as a provider. This woman had to raise the children, pay the bills, keep the family together. Her diary is full of angry references to Jonathan's inadequacies.

"Then Jonathan died, and all the entries ceased except for one — years later. Here it is: 'Today I was made superintendent of schools, and I suppose I should be very proud. But if I knew that Jonathan was out there somewhere beyond the stars, and if I knew how to manage it, I would go to him tonight.' "

The Old Man closed the book gently. "You see? What she's saying is 'if only; if only,' I had accepted him, faults and all; if only I had loved him while I could." He put the book back on the shelf. "That's when those sad words are the saddest of all: when it's too late to retrieve anything."

He stood up a bit stiffly. "Well, class dismissed. It has been good to see you young man. Always is. Now, if you will help me find a taxi, I probably should be getting on home."

We came out of the building into the rainy night. I spotted a cruising cab and ran toward it, but another pedestrian was quicker.

"My, my," said the Old Man slyly. "If only we had come down ten seconds sooner, we'd have caught that cab, wouldn't we?"

I laughed and picked up the cue. "Next time I'll run faster."

"That's it," cried the Old Man, pulling his absurd hat down around his ears. "That's it exactly!"

Another taxi slowed. I opened the door for him. He smiled and waved as it moved away. I never saw him again. A month later, he died of a sudden heart attack, in full stride, so to speak.

Nothing is more desirable than to be released from an affliction, but nothing is more frightening than to be divested of a crutch.

JAMES BALDWIN

122

Much time has passed since that rainy afternoon in Manhattan. But to this day, whenever I find myself thinking "if only," I change it to "next time." Then I wait for the almost-perceptible mental click. And when I hear it, I think of the Old Man.

A small fragment of immortality, to be sure. But it's the kind he would have wanted.

ON YOUR OWN

BY

SUE MONK KIDD

*B*oxes are strewn across the floor of my son's room in various stages of packing. Two suitcases lie open on the bed. I stand in the doorway as Bob sorts through the items in his room, deciding which ones he'll take to college.

Bob picks up a Dr. Seuss book he received weeks earlier as a graduation gift. Its title is *Oh, the Places You'll Go!* He ponders it a moment, then puts it back on the shelf. "Dr. Seuss?" he says. "That's for children!"

There was a time when my son would have done somersaults for a Dr. Seuss book. Somewhere in the garage is a whole box of them, along with other discarded remnants of his childhood.

I let out a sigh, wondering if he's ready to be on his own. I wonder if *I'm* ready for him to be on his own. Bob pulls his baseball glove from the closet. "Do you know where my baseball cleats are?"

"I'll look in the garage." I search in several places without any luck. But in an old box I find a minnow net that I bought four-year-old Bob when his father, Sandy, and I took him for a vacation by the sea.

That summer Bob and I had a ritual. We went to the beach first thing every morning, spread out our towel and read Dr. Seuss's *One Fish Two Fish Red Fish Blue Fish.* Then I would say, "Ready to catch red fish and blue fish?" Off Bob would go along the shore with his new minnow net, skimming for fish. I'd tag right behind him, as if sewn to his shadow.

Now I wander back into Bob's room. "Did you ever read that Dr. Seuss book you got for graduation?" I ask. He shakes his head.

"Me neither," I say, pulling it off the shelf, thinking of the way I read to him on the beach that long-ago summer. I read out loud:

Congratulations!
Today is your day.
You're off to Great Places!
You're off and away! . . .
Oh, the places you'll go!

The rhymes are about a young fellow setting out into life, traveling to amazing places and experiencing amazing things, *all on his own.* Bob edges over. He peers across my shoulder at a picture of this fellow facing several menacing gremlins.

All alone!
Whether you like it or not,
Alone will be something
you'll be quite a lot.
And when you're alone, there's a
very good chance
You'll meet things that scare you
right out of your pants . . .

But on you will go
Though the weather be foul.
On you will go
Though your enemies prowl.

As I read, Bob chuckles. I chuckle too. The heaviness I've been feeling begins to fade.

And will you succeed?
Yes! You will, indeed!
(98 and 3/4 percent guaranteed.)

When I close the book, I notice that Bob's eyes are fired with eager anticipation. I stare at the title of the book: *Oh, the Places You'll Go!* A thought as luminous as the swirling colors on the cover suddenly fills my mind. *This time the shoreline Bob will walk is life itself. If he's going to become truly whole and independent, he needs to walk it on his own, without me tagging behind.*

The next afternoon Bob, his father and I drive to the campus. It takes six trips to Bob's dormitory room to haul all the things he's brought. Finally — too quickly — it's done.

About 50 pieces of motherly wisdom I want to bestow occur to me. I have a particular urge to mention that he should not wear short sleeves in 30-degree weather, or skip breakfast, or wait until the last minute to write his term papers. But these are "gremlins" he'll have to face on his own.

We walk down the steps in silence, pausing beside the car, trying to figure out how to say good-by. His dad grabs him and gives him a hug. I do too. Turning him loose is nearly the hardest thing I ever did in my life. "You'll be fine," I tell him.

Sandy and I stand on the sidewalk and watch him walk away. At the corner of the dorm he looks back over his shoulder and waves. I swallow hard, smile and give him a thumbs-up sign.

That night I take the minnow net from the garage, carry it into Bob's room and hang it on the wall beside his high-school senior picture. I stare at them both a long while, pondering the seasons of love in a mother's life, knowing there's a time to tag along and a time to wave good-by, a time to hold on and a time to let go.

"Oh, son," I whisper, "the places you'll go!"

One doesn't discover new lands
without consenting to lose
sight of the shore for a very
long time.

ANDRÉ GIDE

AND A CHILD SHALL LEAD THEM

BY

HENRY HURT

$\mathcal{B}$lack as the tropical night, the cat patted gently at shadows dancing from the oil lamp's flickering orange flame. Made from a small jar with a wick of tightly twisted paper, the lamp sat on a table beside the bed where eight-year-old Rona Mahilum was sleeping. Nearby, five of her brothers and sisters nestled on woven mats, making the two-room, wood-and-thatch hut a peaceful cocoon of sleeping children.

They were alone in a vast night on the edge of civilization, high up a mountain on the Philippine island of Negros Occidental, 300 miles south of Manila. The children's parents, Rolando and Nenita, along with two older children, had set off along the jagged paths earlier that day last May to sell bread and coffee at a fiesta in Alimatok, a village over an hour away on foot.

In the isolation of the Mahilum hut, the soft glow of lamplight had brought comfort to Rona and the other children as they drifted off to sleep. But now, deep into the night, blazing oil suddenly spilled onto Rona's bed and splattered the floor.

Rona jumped up. She knew instantly that the meddlesome cat had knocked over the lamp. Hearing sizzling, she realized that her shoulder-length hair was on fire. The blaze leapt to her nightclothes.

Rona hit at the flames searing her head and shoulders. Safety was but a step to the door. Then, in the terrifying light, she saw her brothers and sisters stirring.

With flames in her hair, her nostrils filled with smoke, Rona grabbed the first child she could, five-year-old Cheryl. She rushed down the ladder steps into the yard, where she laid the child under the big banana tree. Then she ran back through the smoke, squinting and holding her breath, and lifted both Ruben, four, and Rhocelle, one, to safety.

The initial flash of flame had died down, and the fire had begun its slow, serious business of spreading through the house. Rona entered again, then carried Roberto, seven, outside. Dazed and coughing, he watched as his sister, her hair and clothes still smoldering with smoke and small flames, ran back into the house for nine-year-old Roda. Unable to lift her, Rona frantically pushed her older sister to the window and rolled her out.

With all the children rescued, Rona grabbed the family's plastic pail, ran to the nearby stream and returned to the house to douse the flames again and again. Finally her small body was overcome, and she collapsed facedown in the charred, smoking rubble.

Dark-haired, with bright, smiling brown eyes, Rona Mahilum had worked alongside her mother in the sugar-cane fields since the age of four. Rona worked from dawn to dusk, but no matter how tired she became, she remained cheery—laughing, singing and playing mischievous tricks.

She was an excellent worker, always willing to help others. Quick and smart, she scurried through the fields, her little hands snatching

weeds from among the cane stalks. Her diligence did not go unnoticed. Soon her daily wage of five pesos was increased to eight pesos (30 cents). For a child to get a raise was unusual, and her parents were proud.

When Rona turned six, her mother cut back her work in the cane fields so she could attend school three days a week. The teachers spoke well of Rona, often mentioning her good nature. To Nenita nothing was more important for her children than the chance to learn to read and write.

A better life: that was the theme of Nenita's every hope for her children, as she and Rolando struggled to keep them in school and get them to Mass at the church three miles away in the tiny settlement of Divina Colonia. Such aspirations stood as a beacon over their living conditions, as did the manner in which Nenita lived her own life—sacrificing to give her children advantages, however small, that her own parents never dreamed of.

Now, as she negotiated the long, dark path home, lighting her way with a small oil lamp, Nenita's thoughts were hopeful. She had left Alimatok around midnight, securing a few pesos at the fiesta. Her husband and older children would be along later.

Then she smelled something burning. "Not regular wood smoke," she says. "Smoke that meant something else." She moved more quickly, nearly running as she came into the clearing and saw her house.

The hut was gutted, its roof nearly gone. Beneath the banana tree lay her children—all but one.

"Where's Rona?" Nenita screamed.

"I don't know," Roda answered groggily.

Frantic, Nenita clambered over the collapsed doorway of the hut, her nostrils filled with the odor of burnt flesh and hair. Holding up her lamp, she looked at the devastation. There was no sign of Rona.

Desperately Nenita began digging through the rubble. A black, round hump, like a pile of charcoal, caught her eye. Praying it was not her daughter, Nenita crouched down.

It *was* Rona, pulled up into a ball, facedown. Most of her hair was burned off. A thick, black crust, split by ugly cracks, covered her back and scalp.

Rona had not shown a flicker or a twitch. Nenita felt for a pulse but found none. Weeping, she cried out in her native Ilonggo, "God, I entrust my child to you!" She then carried her daughter from the house and laid her on a large green banana leaf.

"Rona is dead," Nenita told the other children. Overcome by weeping, she lay down, holding Rona's limp hand and begging God to give life to her child. Could he possibly hear such a small voice from such a tiny speck of the universe?

Rona's father, Rolando, returning home toward morning, accepted the news of his daughter's death as God's will. He offered to dig a grave near the house. But Nenita could not yet accept that God would put such a wonderful child on earth only to allow her to die.

For reasons not entirely rational, she decided to take Rona down the mountain to the village of Bato, some six hours away on foot, where there was a small hospital. Perhaps a doctor would at least confirm there was no life in her little girl. *Yes,* she thought, *I will go as soon as the sun is up.*

In the morning sunshine Rona's wounds were wretched to behold. Her left ear was a tiny nub of charcoal. Heavy, black crust covered her back and head, oozing fluid.

Nenita gingerly washed the soot from the girl's face, which somehow had been spared the flames. Even though she believed Rona was beyond pain, she didn't want to carry the child in a fashion that would rub her burns. Nenita positioned her daughter upside down—her belly against her mother's back, her face against her mother's upper legs. The child's

The loving God never forsakes a hero on earth if his courage fail not.

ANDREAS

133

feet hooked over her mother's shoulders, allowing Nenita to grasp them as she walked.

Alone, she trudged along the steep, jagged paths, along soaring hills and precipitous valleys. Midmorning she reached Alimatok, the scene of the previous night's fiesta. There she located her daughter Christina, 14, who had spent the night with a friend.

Now she and Christina walked on toward the next village of Santiago, their sure steps avoiding sharp rocks and knee-deep wash ruts.

A heavy rain broke loose in midafternoon. Cold drops slammed down, battering Rona's encrusted back. Christina held up huge banana-tree leaves for cover. Finally the sad little entourage stopped to wait out the storm.

As she slid Rona off her back, Nenita saw that the child's eyes were open and looking at her. "Momma," came a small voice, "where are we?"

A glorious shiver ran through Nenita's body. "We're going to see a doctor," she said gently. Her spirit soared as she thanked God for such an overwhelming blessing. Then she called out joyfully to Christina, "Rona is alive!"

"Yes," came the small voice again. "I'm alive now, but I'll probably be dead again."

Now that Rona had regained consciousness, her pain was terrible. There was no more resting for Nenita, who again positioned Rona on her back and set out through the rain and mud with ever greater purpose.

Dr. Agnes Bustillo was in her quarters at the small one-story hospital when word came that she was needed. It was just before 7 p.m. Examining Rona, Bustillo found she had third-degree burns over her scalp and back. Her left ear was virtually gone. The burns were over 15 hours old, and infection was mounting.

"It is remarkable that Rona has lived this long," Bustillo told Nenita, but the girl needed to be in the hospital. "If she is not admitted, she will die."

Explaining that her family did not have money, Nenita asked that Rona simply be given first aid. Even for that, she'd have to borrow the pesos to pay. "I cannot throw away the future of all my children to help just one," she said forcefully.

This discussion took place in front of Rona, whose eyes showed she understood—and agreed. Treatment for her could mean no more schoolbooks for her brothers and sisters.

Indeed, life in Negros Occidental was rife with harsh choices. But under no circumstances was Dr. Bustillo going to let Rona go without treatment. She assured Nenita that the bill would not be burdensome.

Bustillo was impressed by how cheerful Rona was in spite of her terrible pain. After four days, though, the doctor insisted Rona be transferred to the more modern hospital in Bacolod, 50 miles away.

The burn treatments were agonizing. Worse, as her back and head healed, horrible scars shortened her shoulder and neck muscles, pulling her head into a hunched position.

A local newspaper and radio station had carried stories about the courageous little girl who was burned saving her brothers and sisters, and funds were raised to help pay the hospital bills. So in June, Rona and Nenita left the hospital with some simple medicines for her wounds and set off on the long journey home. There Nenita went back to work, struggling to pull together pesos for the children to go to school.

As she helped tend the family garden and fetched water from the spring, Rona's smiling bright eyes never faded. She delighted in her brothers and sisters, and they in her. But no amount of good cheer could obliterate the crippling effect of her injuries.

July turned into August, and the medication began to run low. Because of the constrictions in her shoulders, Rona's gait grew ever more halting and clumsy. But a return to the hospital for reconstructive surgery was completely beyond the Mahilums' finances. Nenita prayed that God would do what she could not: help her child.

On a Sunday afternoon in mid-August, the mayor of Manila, Alfredo Lim, sat at home reading an editorial in the newspaper *Today*. A tall, graying man of Chinese ancestry, Lim felt his eyes fill with tears.

His city had recently voted to give an award to a Filipino boxer who had just taken a silver medal at the Olympics in Atlanta. The man seemed to snub the city by not accepting the money. Now the newspaper had a solution.

It urged Mayor Lim to give the money to someone who really deserved the gold: a little girl who three months before had won her scars and her honor not in a boxing ring but in a ring of fire.

A tough former cop and police official, Lim had gained the sobriquet "Dirty Harry of the Philippines" for his war against prostitution, drug dealing and other crime. He proclaimed an undying commitment to protect the innocent. And, says one longtime observer, "he almost never uses normal channels."

Now Lim began calling the editorial office of *Today*, but no one he spoke to that Sunday knew the exact whereabouts of the burnt child. So he did, for him, the next logical thing: he chartered a plane.

Nenita was scrubbing clothes in the river when people came running to say the police were looking for her at home. Strange men in uniform were rarely seen so far up in the mountains. What the police said also

> *Courage is the first of human qualities, because it is the quality that guarantees all others.*
>
> SIR WINSTON CHURCHILL

seemed incomprehensible: the mayor of Manila was on his way to see her. He also wanted to see Rona.

After frenzied discussion Nenita walked home to find Rona. Along with the policemen, the two started the long journey down the mountain—this time not on foot but on board a truck.

When they reached the tall grandfatherly mayor, he leaned down to Rona's level, and her smiling eyes immediately captivated him. He could see that heavy red scars covered her neck and back, that the healing was pulling her shoulders upward, that she couldn't raise her left arm.

"I want to take you both to Manila," he told Rona and her mother.

In Manila, doctors began a series of surgeries to reconstruct Rona's shoulder and neck muscles. Skin grafts went a long way toward removing her scars. The city of Manila paid all medical expenses.

Gifts amounting to 2.7 million pesos ($100,000) were given to the family. Most of it will be held in trust for the education of the Mahilum children.

Rona's dream is to become a teacher. Mayor Lim doesn't see how she can ever be a better teacher than she has been already. "We had to protect this little girl so that her spirit could be celebrated," he said. "If everyone would follow her example, we would live in a beautiful world."

Rona faced the medical procedures with the same courage she had when facing the fire. Asked about her extraordinary bravery, she speaks with a simplicity as profound as her mother's faith. "I did it because they are my brothers and sisters, and I love them."

PAPA WAS AN AMERICAN

BY
LEO BUSCAGLIA

As I entered junior high, Papa and Mama, whom I had loved without question, suddenly became an embarrassment. Why couldn't they be like other parents? Why didn't they speak without accents? Why couldn't I take peanut-butter-and-jelly sandwiches in my school lunches, rather than calamari. (Yuck, the other kids said, he eats squid legs!) There seemed no escape from the painful stigma I felt in being Italian, the son of Tulio and Rosa. "Buscaglia" — even my name became a source of distress.

One day, as I left school, I found myself surrounded by a group of boys. "Dirty dago!" they shouted. "Your mom's a garlic licker, and you're a son of a dirty wop. Go back where you came from!"

It seemed an eternity before I was released from the circle of pushes, punches and taunts. I wasn't really certain what the epithets meant, but I felt their sting. Humiliated and in tears, I broke free and dashed home. I locked myself in the bathroom, but I couldn't stop the tears. What had happened seemed so wrong, yet I felt helpless to do anything about it.

Papa knocked on the door. "What's the matter?" he asked. "What is it?"

I unlatched the door, and he took me in his arms. Then he sat on the edge of the bathtub with me. "Now tell," he said.

When I finished the story, I waited. I guess I expected Papa to immediately set off in search of the bullies or at least find their parents and demand retribution. But Papa didn't move.

"I see," he said quietly. "They finally found you. Those cowards who don't know us but hate us all the same. I know they hurt you, but what they did wasn't meant just for you. It could have been anyone who is different."

"I hate being Italian!" I confessed angrily. "I wish I could be *anything* else!"

Papa held me firmly now, and his voice had an edge of anger. "Never let me hear you say that again! Italians make beautiful music, paint wonderful pictures, write great books and build beautiful buildings. How can you not be proud to be an Italian? And you're extra lucky, because you're an American too."

"But I don't want to be different!" I objected. "I'd rather be like everyone else."

"Well, you're not like everyone else. God never intended us all to be the same. And would you want to be like the boys who hurt you?"

"No."

"Then wipe your tears and be proud of who you are. You can be sure it won't be the last time you'll meet such people. Feel sorry for them, but don't be afraid of them. We've got to be strong."

He dried my tears. "Now," he said, "let's get some bread and butter and go eat in the garden."

Papa came to America in 1911, leaving behind in Montalenghe, Italy, his young wife, year-old child and the only existence he had ever

known. The plan was that Papa should go to Gallup, N.M., and work in the mines until he had accumulated enough money to send for his family. He would amass a small fortune, educate his children, then return to his village to live out his remaining years in dignity. It did not quite work out that way.

The stark reality of the damp, dark mines hardly proved the opportunity Papa had envisioned. It wasn't long before he borrowed some money and set off for Los Angeles, where he found a job as a dishwasher in a small restaurant. Soon he was promoted to waiter and then to maitre d'.

Mama arrived in America a year later. She was detained on Ellis Island until her small son recovered from the measles, and feared that Papa would give up on her. But Papa met every train from New York for weeks until she finally descended into his arms on the train platform in Los Angeles.

Mama immediately took over the management of their modest, two-room house, her first real home. She took in washing and ironing and, like Papa, worked day and night. Soon there were more children, a larger home and, finally, a new-found feeling of security.

I was 14 when Papa announced that he was going to apply for his U.S. citizenship. He joined a night class to improve his English and prepared in earnest for his naturalization exam. He bought a large notebook, writing paper and a dictionary. He picked his clothes for the first class with great care. He even got a haircut.

Papa loved being a student. Every evening he would gather his books and papers and settle in to do his homework. He read and reread citizenship study guides.

It wasn't long before Papa could recite the Pledge of Allegiance and the Preamble to the Constitution. He memorized the Bill of Rights and, much to our amazement, learned the names, in order, of the first 32 Presidents of the United States. He insisted that we quiz him in every spare moment, and he rattled off the answers before we could finish the questions.

Who discovered America? "Cristoforo Colombo, in 1492."

Who were the Pilgrims? "Some nice-a people who came, like me and Mama, to America on a boat, da *Mayflower,* in 1620."

He would use his new-found knowledge to enrich casual conversations with family and friends. "Don't forget," he'd say,"dis is a government of da, by da and for da people."

Papa loved his teacher and was very popular in class. He was given a certificate for being the only member of his class who could recite the Gettysburg Address without a single error. He received honorable mention for his short speech titled "Why I Came to America."

At last, Papa was ready to take his final exam. This was a tense time in our household. For days before he was to appear at the Los Angeles Federal Building for his exam, we all walked on eggs.

So it was with great relief that we watched Papa leave the house, with his two required witnesses, to take the exam. No sooner had he left than Mama started praying.

"Don't worry, Mama," we assured her. "Papa knows everything. He knows more than the examiner." We would not allow ourselves even to imagine what our home would be like if Papa failed.

When he returned, his face was lit with the unmistakable light of success. I can still see him striding triumphantly up the walkway in what was undoubtedly one of the proudest moments of his life. Papa's victory was made all the sweeter because the examiner had singled him out for special recognition. He had commented on Papa's fine preparation and had observed that he was going to make an outstanding citizen.

Still, Papa was a little disappointed that he had not been asked enough questions. After all his studying and worry, only three things were asked of him: What is the highest court in the land? Who was the third President of the United States? What is a democracy? His preface to each of his responses was "That's a easy one."

The swearing-in ceremony was all that was left to make Papa, at last, a real citizen. With hundreds of others, he was required to take the oath of allegiance. We all dressed in our Sunday best, squeezed into our dilapidated car and drove to the courthouse.

The citizens-to-be and their families were separated, and Papa was soon lost in a crowd of people whose cultural diversity seemed less important than their shared accomplishment. I remember very little about the ceremony itself except for the moment in which Papa spotted us in a sea of spectators and waved happily, elated upon becoming a new citizen.

Afterward, we all hugged him with congratulations. "You see," he said, "I'm an American now." He paused for a moment and became very pensive. Then he added, looking straight at me: "Of Italian descent!"

Of course, Papa hadn't solved the problem of bigotry that sunny California day long ago when we ate bread and butter in the garden— or even by becoming a citizen. But his example of pride and determination taught me what an American is. Now I know that acceptance, understanding—and true patriotism—can come only from the strong.

Don't be afraid to go out on a limb.
That's where the fruit is.

H. JACKSON BROWNE

SUMMER OF THE FISH

BY

JACK CURTIS

"Only a sentimental piece of California real estate." Father paced impatiently through the vandalized lodge. He still wore his New York gray suit and black bow tie.

"It's beautiful." Mother's voice held a challenge of stubborn exactitude. "We are keeping it, George."

"It's not my fault your parents couldn't count money." Father returned to the littered living room to face her.

"They could count it," Mother replied. "They just couldn't pinch it."

We'd come three thousand miles to bicker.

Mother took her cane and pegged out on the stone porch that faced the long lake. The lower half of the building was built of gray-and-white river stones carefully fitted together, endowing the cabin with a cool, enduring solidness that bespoke of a people who obviously believed in the future.

Mother took a deep breath of sweet piney air and gazed out over the glittering lake. A grand smile warmed her snub-nosed face. "I

144

should never have left here," she said. "I loved it, and I took strength from it, and I caught fish like poems out of these waters."

Florence Curtis wasn't stupid or flighty. She had a Ph.D. in literature and three published books of poetry. What's more, she'd raised four children and none of us was in jail or on welfare. And my father adored her.

"George," she said, "I think the lodge can be made livable by the first of June. After all these years, I intend to summer here."

"But Florence, it's so damned far from home!" said Father. "What will you do here?"

"Write and fish, fish and write, they're all the same."

Accepting defeat, Father squared his shoulders and went off to make arrangements for the restoration. But my older two brothers and sister fought the decision as if Mother had lost her mind. Harry, the neurosurgeon, thought he'd have the problem sutured and healed in minutes.

"Mother," he said, "you know the tumor cells in your knee may metastasize, flare up, at any moment. There are no facilities out there for proper treatment of a person with bone cancer. All you have to do is knock that knee on something, bruise it, and all hell could break loose!"

"Harry, have you ever fished?"

"I don't fish. I jog. And I'm in excellent shape."

"But you're stuffy. What good is shape if you don't enjoy it, dare it, challenge something grand?"

"I 'm talking hard facts."

"You're talking death when there is still life."

Like the others, Harry was defeated. In the end, it was agreed that Mother would indeed spend the summer at Concord Lake, and I with her. We would leave right after my final exams.

As the family dispersed, Father took me aside. "Anything at all happens, you'll call me, won't you, Jay?"

"Sure," I promised.

We landed in Fresno and then drove northeast out of the smog and urban sprawl. Once in the rising spring-green hills, Mother's mood lifted to euphoria. The air freshened and shared the flavor of conifers as we came into the mountains. Cresting a ridge, Mother pointed to a weathered way station where her parents had always stopped. "Pull in, Jay. Let's have a beer."

It was going to be a crazy summer.

A pine-board dance floor separated the old mahogany bar from a blackened stone fireplace. On the log walls hung old photographs of fishermen displaying extra-large catches of trout or bass.

"Jaybird, look here," exclaimed Mother. "That's me!"

And indeed there she stood—a tanned, disheveled little girl, without a smile, holding a string of huge bass toward the camera.

"How solemn I was," she said. "I was a fanatic in those days. Out at dawn and every twilight." She tilted her bottle and smacked her lips. "Come on, Jaybird. I can't wait!"

We arrived at twilight and sat on the refurbished porch watching the lake go dark. Offshore, a bass rose suddenly after a hatch of white flies, reaching, extending, until he was completely airborne; then, with slapping tail and open mouth, he found his space again.

Mother froze, staring at the ripples, alert as a pointing bird dog, her smile as tense as a do-or-die gun-fighter walking down Main Street. "I have to have a boat I can handle alone, Jay," she said. "And I'll want a good fly rod and reel, tapered line, leaders, and some well-tied dry flies."

Next morning I followed her through the valley's best sporting-goods store, dazed at her vast and precise knowledge of fly-fishing. We bought the works—aluminum pram, small motor, everything she needed.

Courage from hearts and not from numbers grows.

JOHN DRYDEN

Back at the lake, she practiced her casting until dark. When she came inside, a warm exhilaration blotted out the deep lines around her great eager eyes, and a special glow of expectancy flushed her cheeks.

I went with her the first time to be sure she could handle the boat.

"Damn it, Jaybird, I'll not be treated like an invalid," she fussed.

"You know, but I don't know, so show me," I challenged back.

She pointed us into a little cove in the quiet blue morning, cut the motor and cast the fly. It seemed to me she had miles of line ballooning in giant flexing arcs. Her rocking wrist touched the fly to surface, teased it a moment, retrieved and arced it to itch another sensitive spot. The water boiled as a bass tried too late for the fly, but in a second the fly had fallen in the same spot and the fish grabbed the lure. Her smile was a wondrous picture as she played him, easing him to us, letting him play back, until he came spent to her net.

She caught two more before the sun had crested the mountains, and we went in for a fresh-fish breakfast.

From then on she seemed to isolate herself in an intimate routine of fishing and writing. In the late evening we often sat quietly on the front porch to watch the moon rise behind the mountains. Owls tried to start their prey with a careful cadence of hoots, and on the ridge the coyotes sang.

The summer days flowed by like moonlight on long waters. She wrote Father, worked on her poetry, fished every day. I did not suspect that she hunted for one spectacular fish until one morning when I was painting the trim on the back porch and noticed some old pencil lines on the molding. The first set of lines was easy to decipher. Each mark from about four feet high on up, spaced about an inch apart, bore the same date, June 4, the year ascending with the lines. And as June 4 was Mother's birthday, I could imagine her parents marking each year's growth, until she stood five feet, five inches in 1937.

The other marks, those down close to the floor, were not so easy. The first one, about eight inches off the floor, was dated 8/3/29, and beside it was scrawled her nickname: FLO.

Each year after that had a higher line, until the last and highest line read: 7/17/36 SUBLIME! FLO. Obviously, she'd measured her best bass each year, and marked them as she herself was marked. But it didn't add up: 1937 was the end of her growing. But 1936 the end of her fishing? Surely she'd fished in the summer of 1937, when she turned 18. No fish that summer to be remembered? Why?

While sitting on the porch that night, I had the impression that Mother wished to speak of something intimate. I waited.

"Jaybird, I was thinking of when I was a growing-up girl with a bone disease," she said quietly. "A potential amputee."

"But your leg healed?"

"Yes, they cut a piece out of the knee, and put in the gimp." She paused, and sighed, a low groan from the past; then she rose and pegged toward the door. "Jaybird, it's very hard to be a crippled girl. Goodnight."

As the days stacked into weeks, she caught fish enough, but never the one she wanted. At first it didn't matter because of the fun, and the challenge. But as we passed into August, her fun became more of an angry war containing two battles. The first was to sweep every cove with her teasing fly; the second was to maintain her own strength.

Not once did she show a sign of pain, a symptom of inflammation. She completely fooled me until I began to notice her knuckles go white when she leaned on the cane. And her smile seemed a little too set.

Toward the end of the month, I happened to be standing in the shadows as she came up the steps, and I saw the grimace of pain contort her face as she dragged her bad leg along like a keg of fishhooks. I met her on the porch and looked her in the eye, and she knew I knew. "All right," she said bitterly. "The knee is inflamed."

"We promised to call Poppa if anything went wrong."

"Don't be a rat fink, Jaybird."

She settled grimly into a deck chair as night came across the lake. She'd decided to tell it, and get it out.

"Picture the growing girl, juices flowing in her every summer more and more. In those days every girl had to get married, have a family, or be put on the shelf as a dried-up auntie, and that bad knee just wasn't much of a beau-catcher. I put all that girlish juice and passion into fishing this lake. I loved it, but there was always that nagging inside that time was going by."

"And then you met Poppa."

"The Summer of '37. He wasn't interested in fishing, but he found a quality he liked in me, and I saw my mate in him. All that summer I'd been fishing for the big one, the uncatchable challenge every honest fisher goes for. George was going back to Yale, and on his last night here we had a date. I was pretty sure he was going to make a serious commitment, and I was pretty sure I'd accept it. But I went fishing anyway.

"I was still out on the lake when I heard George's car horn. I was an hour late already, but I decided to try one more cast. A two-foot-long bass came standing on his tail to meet my fly. All I had to do was let the fly fall into his open mouth. But the horn was honking, and somehow I decided that it'd be dishonest to hurry such a fish. So I popped the fly away from him and he fell back with a great splash. Then I put the motor on full throttle and blasted home to catch a fella, get married and have my family. I never got to go fishing again until this summer."

It was too dark to see her face, but there was a wetness in her voice. "Jaybird, I want very much to catch that fish or his next of kin."

"Your leg?"

"It's my leg, my pain—and my pleasure out on the lake."

The next day I found a high rock near the house. Through binoculars, I watched her work the shoreline, cove by cove. She stood in the boat, her left hand on the cane, casting with smooth, immaculate arcs.

Autumn was already in the air on the late afternoon when she decided to fish near the island. The good little pram purred across the water, and I settled back on tile rock to keep my secret watch, knowing that it was simply a matter of days before I'd have to call Poppa.

She shut down the motor, clambered up into her awkward tripod position and started laying out the line. The lovely loops were poetry in themselves. But the air was chilling as the sun dropped to the west and the long shadows of mountains crept out like gray cats.

She'd reached the point of rock just opposite my perch when I saw her head come up, body fix taut, alert, and saw the great fish leap from a boil by the rock just as the fly dropped softly into his greedy mouth. His leap continued on high into a grandstand curl and twist, and Mother let him have the line loose until he touched water once again, and then she hit him three times, setting the hook hard and well.

The fish worked her round and round the boat, diving, running, kicking and rocketing up in angry bucking-bronco sunfishes. He gave her no respite. She settled down on the center thwart so that she couldn't be pulled overboard and played him for 15 minutes without gaining a foot of line.

"Are you okay?" I called across into the gathering shadows.

"Hell, yes!" she yelled back.

Another five minutes, and both had weakened. The bass was not standing on his tail anymore, and she was leaning more heavily on the gunwale for support.

After a while her voice floated back weakly. "I'll need a light."

Why hadn't I thought?

I drove the car to the dock and parked it so the headlights shone toward the island, outlining her tortured figure.

"All right?"

"Fine." Then, "He's coming!"

I could see her posture alter. She sat straighter and her hands were moving. The bass no longer splashed. She set the rod aside and leaned over, reaching both hands into the water. Then she settled back with her head bowed for a moment. And then she headed home. As she coasted into the dock, I touched her shoulder. "You okay, Momma?"

"He is such a fine, strong fish," she said. "He was worth it all."

"You let him loose."

"I had him in my hands, that was enough. He measures from the rivet in the oarlock to a scratch I made in the side with my ring."

I lifted her birdlike body out of the boat and carried her up to the lodge. Too weak to sit in a chair, she asked me to help her to bed. Her face was gray, her voice indistinct and fragile. Her lower right leg was a bulging blue-black horror.

"You overdid it, Momma."

She looked up at me with her great eyes glowing. "No, I just did it. Now I think you'd better call your father and tell him I'd love to see him again soon."

"Then I'll take your measurements from the boat and mark it on the board."

"Yes, please do that. And we'll write beside it: 'Released.'"

Sometimes even to live is an act of courage.

SENECA

151

A SPECIAL SORT OF STUBBORNNESS

BY

JOAN CURTIS

I first met Lamar Dodd over 15 years ago in Athens, Ga., at the Georgia Museum of Art. The museum was hosting an exhibition of his paintings, and everyone in our community was going to be there.

Dodd was a legend in Athens, where he'd inspired a generation of young artists and created, at the University of Georgia, one of the most renowned art departments in the country. But to me he was more than an eminent educator; he was a man who had dared to live his dream, a goal I was still struggling to achieve.

For years I had worked as a management trainer at the state university, but the routine and the bureaucracy had begun to stifle me. Now I faced a crossroads in my career. I could remain where I was, secure but without hope for growth, or I could open my own business, which had long been my secret ambition.

As my husband and I crossed the museum's marble floors, I watched men in dinner jackets and women in chiffon chatting familiarly. Among those confident achievers I felt out of place. In the exhibition room,

152

Dodd stood surrounded by admirers. He wasn't a big man, five-foot-nine or so, but he commanded attention. Fluffy white hair crowned his head, and he leaned on a gold-topped cane.

As we approached, I was struck by the brilliance of Dodd's light-blue eyes. We had talked for only a few moments when I noticed how he focused all his attention on me while he spoke. Something in his manner made me feel strong and included.

I looked at his canvases commissioned by NASA to commemorate space exploration. They were large works filled with dominant lines and splashes of brilliant color. The artist's concepts and powerful movements were as audacious as the exploits they celebrated.

After that night, I didn't expect to see Dodd again. But a week later he telephoned. He invited my husband and me to see sketches for a painting and talk about his work.

Dodd met us at the door of his home and guided us to his studio. In the center stood an easel with a huge canvas. Jars, brushes and palettes of paints rested on a small table to the right of the easel. Hundreds of canvases were tucked in cubbies, and still more filled empty spaces in the room.

Dodd wanted to portray in his painting the emergence of the soul from illness. He talked about how to best create a vision of the turmoil, trial and healing that is at the heart of human existence. He and my husband discussed the images that might capture that vision. "And what do you think, my dear?" he asked me.

He so naturally included me in the discussion that later, over coffee, I found myself talking about my dream to start a business that would allow me to teach and write, the two things I loved most.

"You're frightened," he said matter-of-factly. "I know the symptoms."

"That's hard for me to imagine," I replied.

"Why? I've been frightened all my life," he said. "But courage is no more than cussed stubbornness, and I've plenty of that. It means getting up each day and doing what you have to, going on when circumstances get you down, pushing ahead when others hold you back.

"When I graduated from high school," he continued, "I went to Georgia Tech to study architecture. But my heart wasn't in it. I was trying to please others, not myself. I went home after less than a year feeling like a failure. I stayed in my room."

"How did you break out?"

"I got an offer to teach art in a small Alabama school. Working with young people, I threw off the doubts and fears and plunged into painting. I promised myself I'd work every day, no matter how I felt."

And the rest is history, I thought. I wish it could be that easy for me.

Apparently, however, the rest wasn't history—or easy—for Lamar Dodd. After his year of teaching, he went to New York, where he struggled with loneliness, poverty and teachers who disparaged his work. His life, I discovered, was filled with the same irritations and doubts that plague us all. Still, he managed to overcome the barriers.

Lamar Dodd and I became friends, and I found he had a flintier side. One time it was raining after we had lunched at a restaurant, and Lamar walked me to my car. I then offered to drive him up the hill to his car. "No, no," he replied. "A little rain never hurt anyone."

He wouldn't even take my umbrella. Thinking I could match his obstinacy, I trudged with him to his car, holding the umbrella over his head. Then Lamar declared that it grieved his Southern manhood to let a lady walk alone to her car, and he insisted on returning with me.

So back we passed, to the immense curiosity of some diners under the restaurant's awning. Finally I let him go, dripping like a derelict but with pride intact.

I often visited him at his home, and he always encouraged me to take the dare I was setting for myself. But I still made no attempt to begin the business I dreamed of. Meanwhile, Lamar unleashed a series of brilliant watercolors. The scenes came from memories of sunflowers he had seen in Cortona, Italy, and fishermen off Maine's coast. His imagination and ability to create seemed endless.

Then Lamar had a stroke.

For weeks I feared seeing him again. His right hand, the hand with which he painted, was paralyzed, and along with it, I was sure, his courage crushed.

Finally I went to visit him. I knocked at his door and heard sluggish footsteps approaching. When he opened the screen, I saw the familiar crop of white hair. His eyes were cloudier, but the distinctive gleam was still there.

"Such a pleasure, my dear," he said. His voice was like a recording played slightly off speed. He leaned on the gold-topped cane, his right hand resting on the head. We went into the sitting room adjacent to his studio and talked about many things, but not his devastating transformation. And gradually, like the Southern gentleman he was, he turned the conversation to me, my concerns and ambitions.

Before leaving I visited the powder room. When I returned to say farewell, I found Lamar in his studio. He had shuffled over to his easel and was standing before it in intense concentration. Sitting on the large frame was a magnificent oil painting of an island jutting out of a turbulent blue-green sea. As I watched in silence from the hallway, my heart broke for him. How sad it must be to contemplate the work you can no longer do.

Then something remarkable happened. Lamar picked up a paintbrush in his left hand and inched toward the canvas. He placed the brush in his lifeless right hand. With extreme effort, he trapped the brush between two fingers and rested the shaft against his palm. Then, with his left hand guiding—and with agonizing care—he pushed the brush across the surface, leaving a perfect line of color.

After a few moments, he turned to see me watching. He slowly put down the brush.

"Just try, my dear," he said. "Courage is nothing more than cussed stubbornness." With tears in my eyes, I went over to him, kissed his cheek and found my way out.

My life changed after that visit. I quit my job and opened a small consulting business, just as I had always dreamed. Like Lamar, I faced the challenge of leaving everything behind to chase something unknown. Like Lamar in his early days, I wondered if I could be successful. And like Lamar, who continued to paint until he passed away last year at age 86, I hope I'll overcome the obstacles that life places before me.

My dear friend and mentor was so right about courage being a special sort of stubbornness. And I've since come to understand it's much more. It's the essence of the creative spirit, the vital force of the human heart.

Give us grace and strength to forbear and to preserve. . .

Give us courage and gaiety and the quiet mind,

spare us to our friends, soften us to our enemies.

ROBERT LOUIS STEVENSON

THE HEART OF CANTON, OHIO

BY

HENRY HURT

*P*olice officer David Bober, on late-night patrol in Canton, Ohio, tensed as he heard the radio dispatcher's report: a man had been run over by a train. Bober sped the car toward a railroad crossing downtown. The big switching locomotive sat growling as trainmen with lanterns frantically directed Bober back 500 feet up the dark track bed.

Shining his light under a car, Bober saw the crumpled upper part of a man's body. The legs, severed far above the knees, lay outside the tracks. *Doctors alone could not save this man,* Bober thought. *And even if he survives, what then? . . .*

A week later, Charles Torrence, Jr., 24, emerged from a sporadic coma. His memory of the traumatic event was foggy. Police believe that Torrence, then a laborer at Republic Steel, was on his way home after visiting friends. To save time, he swung onto the slow-moving train and somehow fell between the cars.

For a young man with no marketable skills, the future was heavy with gloom. Charlie's family and friends promised perpetual love and care. Doctors spoke of surgery that might fit the small stubs of his legs with artificial limbs. But hovering over this well-intended concern was a pervasive, cloying pity—something Charles Torrence had never known in his tough, independent life. It hammered at a chord of pride deep within him, and played back in quiet resentment.

"I didn't want help from anybody," Charlie Torrence says, 37 years after losing his legs. He speaks with a powerful voice, resonant with pride. "I wanted to see what I could do on my own—just God and me. I never doubted I was going to be all right." His words carry a conviction steeled by his having proved his point.

Divorced and without children, Charlie did not have to worry about dependents. He was eligible for Social Security disability. His goal was to live a normal life—at least those parts of life he considered important. They had to do, unabashedly, with the heart. And Charlie Torrence did not need his legs for that. Nor did he need legs to win the heart of this old northeastern Ohio town.

One of the niceties Charlie has refused over the years is a wheelchair. "It wouldn't help me a bit," he says. "I couldn't jump curbs and hop potholes. And it would sit up too high and give me bad balance. It would be worthless for my kind of traveling."

Charlie's kind of traveling has been a source of inspiration and hair-raising concern to the people of Canton for nearly four decades. Charlie travels on an 18-inch-wide homemade cart that sits about five inches off the ground. A padded back comes up to the level of his shoulders. With one wheel on the front and two on the rear, the contraption is put into motion by two semicircular wooden and rubber "walking blocks" powered solely by the strong muscles of Charlie's huge arms and chest. In a kind of rowing motion, he leans forward and clamps the blocks onto the pavement to pull the cart ahead.

Charlie sits soldier-straight, tightly buckled onto his cart. The rich, black skin of his face covers well-chiseled features. His hair is flecked

with gray. His head and eagle eyes are constantly in motion, sweeping the streets. Peering through tinted glasses, those eyes check out anything that moves. As he talks, a pipe billowing smoke juts from his teeth. His words come resolutely, with a bristle to them that puts one on notice that this man brooks no nonsense and asks for nothing. To a stranger, the tough crust around Charlie Torrence is as thick as the calluses on his hands.

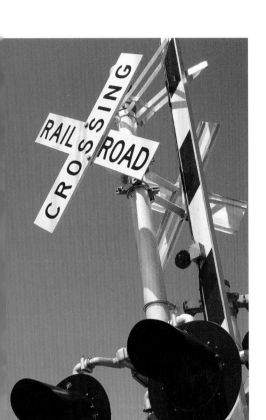

Charlie lives with his sister in their small, wood-frame house about two miles from downtown Canton. Nearly every day he travels to town, crossing the railroad tracks on a pathway not far from where he lost his legs. He shops around for his lunch and, occasionally, joins a friend at the counter. It is said that Charlie can move from his cart to the top of a counter stool so quickly that no one has ever really seen exactly how he does it.

Lunch done, he makes his rounds through the streets. Dozens of people wave to him and speak. He banters merrily with them, generous with advice and philosophy. He may debate with someone about pipe tobacco or discuss something going on at his church. An affectionate warmth fills the air during these encounters—a camaraderie so natural that a visitor resigns himself to remaining an outsider.

He is quick to offer directions to those who seem to need them. Patrolling policemen occasionally stop to chat, and Charlie usually is ready with some report about street or traffic conditions. More than once, when the railroad safety gates have been stuck, Charlie has positioned himself on the tracks to direct traffic.

Some of Charlie's friends are high-school students. "Kids used to get their experience from real life," Charlie says. "Now they get most of it by watching television, which leads to frustration and friction and then to trouble getting along with others. Kids need to live in the real world if they're ever going to be happy and understand how to deal with what comes their way."

If Charlie senses any pity coming his way, he is quick to denounce it. "I'm a lot better off than most people who feel sorry for me," he says. "I just wish they would look at me and try to understand what's in my heart, what makes me go. It could do them some good. I think that's why God kept me around."

What *is* in Charlie Torrence's heart? "Courage, faith and willpower. They're in everybody's heart, but some people don't ever find them in themselves because they spend their time worrying about what they don't have, or complaining. Why, some people even complain about the weather!"

To Charlie, the weather is particularly irrelevant. Rain, snow and cold are simply challenges to his determination to go where he pleases. Jim Hillibish, a reporter for the Canton *Repository* who has known Charlie for years, remembers when he and his wife offered Charlie a ride on a miserable night. "He thanked us and refused," Hillibish recalls. "He said he felt better traveling his own way." Later, Hillibish drove past Charlie, who was pulling himself the four miles home through driving rain.

"I don't like to ride in cars," says Charlie. "It gets me out of rhythm. I know my own pace. I know exactly when I have to leave to get where I'm going, and when I'm going to get there."

The act of *getting there* is a very important part of Charlie's life. It has to do with why he thinks he was spared that night on the railroad tracks. "I like to travel the streets and let people see me," he says. "I want them to see how you can handle anything that comes your way, as long as you are determined you're going to do it. I think it helps people when they see that."

"You'll never count all the lives Charlie has touched," says Walter Kohler, a 25-year veteran of the Canton police department. "People worrying about their problems see Charlie pulling himself along in the bitter cold, and their problems get put into perspective in a hurry."

The Canton police worry that Charlie might get run over and killed, traveling as he does. He has been hit by motorists at least five times, and the last collision a couple of years ago gave him a broken collarbone. The Police Boys Club built Charlie a new cart, and Police Chief Tom Wyatt made sure Charlie got a bright-orange vest. A couple of orange flags now fly from the cart on a six-foot antenna.

Clearly, no one in Canton would even consider trying to alter Charlie's habits. Indeed, he is as prominent a figure as anyone in the town. "The whole city regards him as someone very special," says Mayor Samuel D. Purses. "He shows us the importance of never giving up." Stanley A. Cmich, who served as mayor of Canton for 20 years, simply states, "I believe that every one of our citizens over the years has come to love Charlie for his optimism, for the example he sets. He shows us all that we can and must take control of our lives, no matter what happens to us."

The people of Canton, perhaps, need Charlie's inspiration more than ever. A proud, boisterous old industrial city, Canton has changed dramatically over the past 35 years. She has seen her downtown falter as shopping malls have sprung up in suburbs. Major industries have closed, leaving an unemployment rate higher than the national average. Still, President William McKinley's home and the Pro Football Hall of Fame attract many visitors, and renovation has begun in parts of the downtown area.

Despite her problems, Canton has a richness of heart. It is a heart that has room to cherish and respect a man who has no legs and who pulls himself through the streets on a tiny cart. There is a graciousness, a camaraderie in this ubiquitous regard for Charlie Torrence.

Wait for the Lord; be strong, and let your heart take courage; yea, wait for the Lord!

PSALMS 27

Where do such noble instincts come from? In a sense, Canton's citizens are simply reflecting those values inspired by Charlie Torrence. He made a courageous decision when he declared he would do things his way—alone, with God's help. Against all worldly odds, he has prevailed and shown others something about himself and, he hopes, something about God. Most important of all to Charlie, he has shown them something noble about themselves.

No pain, no palm; no thorns,
no throne; no gall, no glory;
no cross, no crown.

WILLIAM PENN

ORDEAL ON MT. JOHNSON

BY

SHELDON KELLY

David Nyman gazed out over the sunlit white peaks as the chartered ski plane nosed toward the towering Alaska Range. "Great weather!" Dave, 31, yelled to his climbing partner, James Sweeney, 33. Jim smiled and nodded in assent.

Soon the plane entered the Great Gorge, an enclosure of nearly 10,000-foot spires, columns and ice-capped rock faces. The gorge also contained one of the earth's most magnificent sights — the 35-mile-long Ruth Glacier. It was in this virtually impenetrable wilderness, 50 miles from civilization, that Dave and Jim planned to spend ten days climbing.

Jim, a carpenter and ski-rescue-patrol member, had left California for Alaska ten years earlier. Dark and lean, he climbed with passion and trained constantly. Dave, an Anchorage-born engineer, shorter and 20 pounds heavier than his companion, climbed for adventure and fun. He had scaled the Cascades, Rockies, Andes and Alps, but he seldom trained.

Deposited three miles from Mt. Johnson, their ultimate destination, Jim and Dave set up a base camp of two domed tents. For the first five days they honed their skills on the columnar peaks two miles up the glacier. By the morning of April 19, 1989, they agreed they were ready for Mt. Johnson's Elevator Shaft, an ice-encrusted gorge that angled some 2500 feet up the north side of the mountain.

As they set out, both men were wearing helmets, tinted goggles, climbing boots and outerwear made of wind-resistant nylon over polypropylene long johns. Tied to their harnesses were 165-foot lengths of rope; anchors to be driven into rock or ice; snap-on links that attach the rope to the anchors; and figure-eight belay plates, used to rappel or stop a fall.

They ski-trekked through deep snow to an overhang section of the mountain wall. Jim knotted a rope-end to his harness and gave the other end to Dave, who affixed it to his own. Swinging his ice ax and crampons — attached boot claws — into the wall, Jim started moving up. Dave paid out rope from below as Jim climbed the full 165-foot rope length. With an ice ax, Jim hammered several anchors into the wall and tied himself in place. Then Dave started up.

In three hours, the two climbed more than 600 feet up the 75-degree incline. But the snow and ice had become increasingly unsettled, and storm clouds could be seen several miles away. Exhausted, sweating heavily, Dave felt uneasy as he stood on a ledge, while Jim continued to climb above.

Suddenly a huge sheet of snow filled the air, followed by sounds of clanging metal. Instinctively Dave yanked the belay rope into an arrest position as a large object fell past him in a blur, followed by rocks, ice and more sheets of snow. A split-second later he was jerked off his feet by the rope and slammed against the ice wall.

Stunned, Dave hung from the anchor above, seeing nothing but drifting snow. He realized that the blurred object that had plummeted past him must have been Jim. Looking down the rope lines, he saw Jim's upended boots 50 feet below.

Quickly he rappelled to his partner. *He's dead!* Dave thought. Jim's helmet had been cracked like an eggshell. Blood streamed from his nose, mouth and ears, and his eyes were closed. "Jim!" Dave shouted, placing his fingers against his friend's carotid artery. Jim moaned and rolled his eyes. Dave was relieved. But his partner's hip or legs appeared to be broken, and his head injury had left him delirious.

Through the seven years they had climbed together, Jim had shown more technical expertise, and Dave had usually let him lead, agreeing with his routes and tactics. Now Dave realized that the decisions would be his alone, that their survival depended on him.

Quickly Dave anchored three ice screws into the mountain's icy face, clipped his partner onto the new belay and then flipped him upright. Jim stared into the mountain wall. "What happened?" he asked.

"You fell," Dave answered. "I'm taking you down."

"Dave! We've got to keep climbing!" Jim insisted. Dave ignored his partner's rantings as he climbed back up to the lifesaving anchor. Straining every muscle, he transferred the rope holding Jim's leaden weight to the new anchor below. Then, rigging a rappel device, he slid down.

Methodically, Dave began lowering his semiconscious partner. He would slide down the 165 feet, set anchors, fasten Jim in the new belay, go back up to free the rope, then rappel down again.

Occasionally, blinding whirlwinds of powdery snow pummeled them. But Dave worked steadily. Each foot descended became a victory.

Perfect valor is to do without witness what one would do before all the world.

LA ROCHEFOUCAULD

168

After five hours, he had lowered Jim over 600 feet. Yet he hadn't been able to follow their earlier route of ascent. They would have to go another 400 feet straight down onto a hanging glacier beside the Elevator Shaft.

Dave knew he had pushed himself beyond the limits of endurance; he could barely cling to the ice wall. The scudding froth of clouds against the blue sky reminded him that a storm was brewing, nightfall was only hours away and his partner might be dying. At once he was infused with new strength.

Finally Dave lowered Jim to the soft snow covering the glacier. He rappelled down after him. "We made it, you old dog," he said, cradling his partner's head.

Dave now hurried to that morning's bivouac site to retrieve their supplies. At dusk, after Dave had some hot food and tea, the men lay in their down sleeping bags. Jim, who had taken aspirin, was now less confused. Dave felt heartened. He had feared that Jim would go into shock and that fluid would build up inside his skull from his head injury.

Another cause for worry was hypothermia, which attacks a perspiration-soaked body with deadly speed in such temperatures. Dave had dressed Jim in down pants and coat before pulling his bag around him. Although in severe pain, he was warm and dry.

Early the next morning a whirlwind of snow dusted the climbers' bags. Soon they were being buried in wave after wave of blanketing snow. Fearful of avalanches, Dave dragged his partner 100 feet to what he hoped was a safer location. He gave Jim more aspirin, the last dry pair of socks and a bottle of water. Then he placed him inside a sack of weatherproofed fabric and put his own soaked sleeping bag around it, creating an insulation barrier.

Dave, wet and shivering, prepared a hot breakfast, but Jim refused to eat. "The climb's going great," he said, his eyes glazed. Dave knew another relapse into delirium could mean that Jim's condition was deteriorating and without medical treatment he could die that night. "I'm going for help right away!" he told Jim.

Dave's destination — and only hope — was the Don Sheldon Mountain House, a climbers' refuge seven miles away. To get there he'd have to ski through snow fields with many crevasses — deep chasms often hidden by thin bridges of snow. Although traversing crevasse fields alone was very dangerous, there was no other way, and he set off. Some depressions in the snow collapsed an instant after he crossed.

Arriving at the refuge, Dave was ecstatic to find four vacationing skiers. There was no radio at the house. But the group's leader explained that their chartered plane would return in two days and added that he had mountain-rescue experience. Since Dave was too exhausted to return right away, the leader and another skier offered to take supplies to Jim on Mt. Johnson and make him as comfortable as possible. Dave told them to follow his tracks through the crevasse fields and gave them Jim's location. "I'll grab a few hours' sleep," he told the men as they departed. "Then I'll follow you."

Awaking at dawn, Dave left immediately and soon met the two skiers — returning. *Jim is dead!* he thought. As they approached, Dave began shouting questions, and they explained that the glacier was too difficult for them to climb; there had been too many avalanches.

"I'll need the gear and a volunteer," Dave said quietly. The group leader handed over the supplies and equipment; there would be no volunteer. "You'll make it," he said breezily, promising to tell their pilot to radio for help. Skiing back toward Mt. Johnson, Dave repeated over and over, *Damn right I'll make it!*

Snow rolled off the mountain face as Dave approached the hanging glacier. A kaleidoscope of scenes flashed through his mind: finding Jim's stiffened body; Jim, lying in a crevasse, never to be found. He closed his eyes and prayed.

"Help! Help!" Jim's cries echoed off the frozen walls. "I'm coming, Jimbo!" Dave yelled back joyfully. When Dave reached the site, he saw that Jim had been carried some 200 feet by an avalanche and lay buried in snow to his chest.

Later, inside the tent Dave had brought, he again gave Jim aspirin, dressed him in dry clothing and fixed hot food and tea. Until help arrived, they would wait in relative comfort.

Early on the morning of April 23, following a day in which the men had tried to rest, an avalanche hit, burying the tent. Dave had to dig out with his hands. That evening, the temperature dropped, and snow began to fall heavily. The men lay silent in their bags, waiting, praying. They knew that most large avalanches occurred during or after heavy snowfall. Soon the area was filled with sounds of explosions as huge chunks of snow and ice crashed down.

Seventy-five-mile-per-hour winds rocked their anchored tent like a boat on a storm-tossed sea. Dave recited the Lord's Prayer over and over as he strained to hold the aluminum tent poles against collapse. He had never been more frightened in his life. Medical evacuation, he knew, would be impossible in this weather. The storm raged through the night and into the next day.

The men had to shift camp several times. An avalanche buried them in the morning, but, again, Dave was able to dig them out. They were now down to one good sleeping bag, and their food was almost gone.

Hours before dawn on April 25, wind hit with new ferocity, and the tent began to lift. Dave felt himself being propelled through the air like a cannonball. Moments later he lay some 200 feet below their tent site.

Then he heard Jim's voice from nearby: "Dave! I've got the sleeping bag!" But almost all their supplies — including the tent, Jim's boots, the ice ax, their pot for boiling water, their ropes and remaining food — had been lost.

Later, huddled inside a coffin-like hole dug into the snow, the men listened to the shuddering maelstrom of snow, ice and rock. "If you left me," Jim suddenly told Dave, "you could live."

"We leave together," Dave answered firmly.

He rigged a crude sled for Jim by encasing him in the sleeping bag and a camper's utility bag, and harnessing those to an insulation pad. For the next 17 hours Dave dragged his injured partner across crevasses and fragile snow-bridges. They were constantly threatened by avalanches and falling ice.

On the morning of April 26, the climbers heard an awesome rumble. A huge avalanche scooped them up and hurled them toward a gaping crevasse. *Am I really going to die?* Dave thought. *Is this it?*

Swallowed by darkness as he fell into the chasm, he thrust out his legs, digging his boots into the narrow walls, and fell onto a thin ledge. At the other end of the ledge, Jim's bearded, encrusted face was barely visible. Realizing they were both safe for the moment, they began laughing uncontrollably with relief.

After placing Jim in a cavelike shelter, Dave began crawling carefully along the ledge. He knew that such protrusions could shear off at any moment — but they sometimes led to the surface. Indeed, 30 feet away he discovered a steep ramp leading up to the glacier. He returned to get Jim.

To pull his partner up the ramp, Dave held the harness webbing with his teeth. He used one hand to yank Jim on the makeshift sled, the other to make steps in the ice and snow. Dave struggled, inch by inch. A half-

Who bravely dares must sometimes risk a fall.

TOBIAS G. SMOLLETT

172

hour later they reached the glacier surface. Dave's chest was heaving convulsively.

He moved cautiously. Slopes, icy ridges, more crevasses had to be traversed. At one point, Dave had to dig a tunnel through an obstructing snow wall and pull Jim through.

Hours passed. Suddenly a plane flew overhead and tipped its wings. Rescuers had found them! Tears streamed down Dave's face. Their ordeal was finally over.

The climbers were flown to Providence Hospital in Anchorage, where Jim was treated for a severe concussion and underwent surgery for a broken hip. Dave, who lost 25 pounds during the week, was treated for frostbite on his hands.

One of Alaska's leading mountain-rescue experts, Nick Parker, called Dave Nyman's rescue of his partner "the bravest and most selfless action I've seen in a lifetime of climbing." In April 1990, Dave was awarded the Carnegie Medal for extraordinary heroism. But for him, his true reward had come when, shortly after the rescue plane had spotted them, Jim Sweeney softly told him: "You're a hero, Dave. You saved my life."

PLAY IT AGAIN, DAD

BY
LAURA SESSIONS STEPP

From second grade on, there was one event I dreaded every year: the piano recital. A recital meant I had to practice a boring piece of music and perform in front of strangers who, I was sure, knew the notes much better than I. It also meant wearing a crinkly crinoline dress and enduring the bright lights of a movie camera as I swished across the church stage.

Each year I would ask my father if I could skip the recital "just this once." And each year he'd say no, muttering something about building self-confidence and working toward a goal.

So it was with great satisfaction that I stood in church one recent Sunday, video camera in hand, and watched my father sweat in his shirt and tie before rising to play the piano in his very first recital.

Eight-year-old Patrick Gurney led off the event, followed by Susannah Thomson, nine. Then came my 68-year-old dad, Robert Sessions, who sat down at the Kawai grand piano and taught me more about courage and persistence than all the words he used those 30-plus years ago.

174

From the time he was small, my father had longed to play music. His mother, a factory worker, couldn't afford lessons, so a kindly couple in the small Arkansas town where he lived offered to pay. But he soon stopped after being teased by other boys his age. "I quit and always regretted it," he recalls.

He could have gone on regretting it, as too many of us do. But though he was rooted in his past, he wasn't stuck there. Three years ago, when he retired from the faculty at the University of Richmond, he asked his church music director, Charles Staples, to take him as a student. Staples had the good grace not to laugh. Just before the recital, he told me my dad was playing "the best I've ever seen him. I keep waiting for him to reach his peak, but he hasn't yet."

For a moment after my father sat down at the keyboard to play, he simply stared down at his fingers, and I wondered whether he would even begin. He had tried to keep the event quiet, telling my stepmother she didn't need to come. But she had every intention of coming, and also invited my sisters and me as well as my dad's three golfing partners who, much to his dismay, showed up.

As we waited those few seconds, I knew he was worrying that his music would sound, well, juvenile—that we'd expect more from a 68-year-old than an eight-year-old, even someone who had been playing for so short a time. His sense of dignity, a precious commodity at any age, was on the line.

He's forgotten the notes, I worried, remembering those split seconds decades ago when my mind would go blank and my fingers would freeze.

But then the sure, poignant strains of Aram Khachaturian's "Melody" emerged, from the same large fingers that once baited my fishing lines, and I realized he had been doing what music teachers always tell their novitiates to do: focus on the music and pretend the rest of us aren't there.

Also in the audience was my 11-year-old son Jeff. My father has taught his grandson how to play hearts, pitch a tent, cast a fishing rod, swing a golf club and compose music on the computer. He encouraged Jeff to start the piano even when the boy insisted he would never play in a recital; two years ago, Dad was there when Jeff did what he said he would never do.

So somehow it was fitting to hear Jeff offer my father some advice about performing. "Just remember, if you make a mistake, it's not the end of the world," my son told him. "Probably no one will notice it anyway."

My dad made it through "Melody" and sailed through Burgmüller's "Arabesque." What he lacked in precision, he more than made up for in feeling. He then rose, turned to his audience and curtsied, making us laugh with relief and affection.

"So what did you think about your granddad?" I asked Jeff later.

"He was great," Jeff replied. "I'm glad he did it. And I bet he is too."

"I'm proud of him for starting something new at his age," I said.

"Yeah, and doing it so well," Jeff added. "It would be like Dr. Spock taking up baseball at 90. I guess he could do it, but it would be hard."

T. Berry Brazelton, the pediatrician and author, says grandparents show grandchildren the mountaintops while parents teach the drudgery of how to get there. My father may not have reached his peak musically, but as far as his grandson is concerned, he's at the top of the mountain.

In life, as in a football game,

the principle to follow is:

hit the line hard.

THEODORE ROOSEVELT

MESSAGE FROM
THE SEA

BY
ARTHUR GORDON

*S*ome people in this world have a marvelous gift. It's hard to say exactly what this quality is: a serenity, an inner strength, a generosity of spirit. Whatever it is, when you're in trouble, or have some aching problem, you turn to these people instinctively. Something in them draws you like a magnet. I have a friend like that. So, the other night, when something was weighing on my mind, I telephoned him.

"Come on over," he said. "Alma's gone to bed, and I was about to heat up some coffee."

So I went over, and at the end of an hour — just as I knew I would — I felt a lot better. The problem was still there, but somehow it didn't seem so frightening. Not with Ken sitting in his old swivel chair, feet up on the desk, hands locked behind his head, not saying much, just listening . . . and *caring*.

Suddenly the gratitude and affection I felt seemed to need expression "Ken," I said, "when it comes to smoothing out wrinkles in troubled minds, you're wonderful. How do you do it?"

He has a slow smile that seems to start in his eyes. "Well," he said, "I'm a good deal older than you."

I shook my head. "Age has nothing to do with it. There's a calmness in you that goes very deep. Where did you get?"

He looked at me pensively for a few seconds, as if trying to make up his mind whether to tell me something. Finally, with the toe of his shoe, he pulled open one of the desk drawers. From it he took a small cardboard box. He put it on the blotter. "If I do have any of this quality you're talking about," he said, "it probably comes from this." I waited. On the mantel a clock ticked.

Ken picked up one of his blackened pipes and began to load it. "You've know me for — how long? Ten years? Twelve? This box is a lot older than that. I've had it more than 30 years. Alma is the only other person who knows what's in it, and maybe she has forgotten. But I take it out and look at it now and then."

The match flared; the smoke curled, blue and reflective, in the lamplight. "Back in the 20's," Ken said in a faraway voice, "I was a successful young man in New York. Successful as hell. I made money fast and spent it faster. I was the golden boy, able to out-think or out-drink anybody. I married Alma because she was pretty and decorative, but I don't think I loved her. I don't think there was any love in me, really. The closest thing to it was the very high regard that I had—for myself."

I stared at him in amazement. I found it almost impossible to believe this brutal self-portrait.

"Well," said Ken, "as you've probably anticipated, the day of reckoning came. And it was quite a day. It's hard for people who didn't go through the Wall Street crash to know what it was like. One week I was a millionaire — on paper, anyway. The next I was a pauper. My reaction was predictable; I got drunk and stayed drunk for three days."

He gave a short bark of a laugh and stood up, running a hand through his wiry hair. "The place I chose for this little orgy of self-pity was a beach cottage that we owned — or, rather, had owned before the bottom fell out of our gilded cage. Alma wanted to come with me, but I wouldn't let her. I just wanted to get away from everything and drink myself blind, and I did.

"But the time comes when you begin to sober up. For an alcoholic — and I was close to being one — this can be a ghastly experience. You're overwhelmed with self-disgust; you're choked with despair. I looked at my face in the mirror, the bloodshot eyes, the three-day beard, and knew I was looking at a total failure. As a man, as a husband, as a human being, I had made a complete mess of my life. The thought — no, it wasn't a thought, it was a conviction, — the conviction came to me that the best thing I could do for Alma and everyone else would be to remove myself from the scene, permanently.

"I knew, moreover, just how to do it. A half-gale was blowing outside. The sea was wild. I would swim out as far as I could, past the point of no return. That would take care of everything."

Ken's pipe had gone out; he put it on the desk. The old chair creaked as he sat down. "When you're driven to a decision like that, your one thought is to get it over with. So I wasted no time. I stumbled down the porch steps and onto the beach. It was just after dawn, I remember; the sky was red and angry; the waves were furious. I walked straight to the edge of the water. As I reached it, something glinted on the sand." He opened the box. "This."

In the box was a shell. Not a particularly unusual shell; I had seen others like it. A narrow oval of fluted calcium, pale, graceful, delicate.

"I stood there staring at it," Ken went on. "Finally I picked it up, wet and glistening. It was so fragile that the least pressure of my fingers would have crushed it. Yet here it was, undamaged, perfect.

"How was this possible? The question seemed to seize upon my mind, while all around me the wind shrieked and the ocean roared. Tons of seething water had flung the shell on the hard-packed sand. It should have been smashed to splinters, utterly destroyed. But it wasn't.

"What had kept the shell intact and unbroken? I kept asking myself this question with a kind of frantic urgency, and suddenly I knew. It had yielded itself to the awful forces crashing around it. It had accepted the storm just as it had accepted the stillness of the depths where it had had its beginnings. And it had survived. And all at once I saw myself battling against the inevitable, beating my fists against fate, when I should have been accepting, with faith.

"I don't know how long I stood there, but finally, when I turned away from the sea, I took the shell with me. I've had it ever since."

I took the box from my friend and lifted out the shell. It lay in my hand, untouched by the years exquisitely wrought, feather-light. "Do you know its name?" I asked.

Ken smiled that slow smile of his. "Yes," he said. "They call it an Angel's Wing."

AGAINST ALL ODDS

BY

AMY ASH NIXON

As she rushed up the hill toward the brownstone building on a bitter December morning, Bonnie Bentley Cewe prayed that she would not let herself down. For six years she had immersed herself in books to prepare for the next five hours, and it had taken every ounce of determination she had. If she failed now, she wasn't sure she had it in her to try again.

The long gash above her hairline had healed, but the puncture wounds on her hand still showed, and her leg ached inside the brace as she took her seat in the drafty room. As the proctor handed out the law-school admission tests, Cewe wondered how a 34-year-old single mother could compete with the young students around her. Their parents probably put credit cards in their wallets and bought them cars. In her wallet was a week's worth of food stamps.

Who am I kidding? she thought. When she opened the test booklet, her mind raced, and she fought the old fear of failure.

In 1972, when she dropped out of Mark T. Sheehan High School in Wallingford, Conn., Bonnie thought she would never look back. She married and had two sons. For a while she dressed windows for a department store; later she helped her husband with the books for his home-improvement business. But after six years of a stormy marriage, Cewe decided to end it. She didn't want her sons to grow up thinking that kind of relationship was normal.

Three days before Christmas 1983, she moved into an apartment she could barely afford, where she and her sons, then three and four, could start over. Christmas morning, the three gathered in the kitchen. One of the boys asked why they were eating their hot cereal standing up, and the other said, "Because there are no chairs." The simplicity of the answer threw them into fits of laughter.

Cewe was now 29, a high-school dropout on welfare. She could see herself in 15 years, working at a minimum-wage job, her boys having no chance for college.

The thought scared her. She would have to go back to school.

In the divorce, Cewe had lost her house, which had been in her in-laws' name as a safeguard in case her husband's business failed. She felt victimized by the legal system, and she decided to act on a lifelong dream. She would become a lawyer and do as Perry Mason had done — protect the innocent and expose the guilty.

Adult classes at her old high school were a long way from law school, and each time Cewe passed the locker she had used as a teen-ager, she had to fight feelings of failure. But when she finished the year, her grades were nearly perfect. In the spring of 1985, as she walked to the high-school stage in cap and gown, her sons clapped ecstatically.

Earning a high-school diploma gave Cewe a taste of how crammed her life would be and how little money she would have if she went on. Going part time to Albertus Magnus College in New Haven and then part time to law school would take 15 years.

Fifteen years. She couldn't say it with a straight face. She would have to attend full time.

She worked nights, sometimes six or seven a week, as a bartender at a restaurant in nearby Meriden. Occasionally, the burden overwhelmed her. One night, before junior-year final exams, walking through the piles of clothes and toys carpeting the boys' room, she stepped on something and heard it break. Her calm broke, too, and she fled to her room in tears.

An hour or so later, she heard a tap on her door. Close your eyes, her boys said, as they marched her to their bedroom. They had done something special, she knew. *Boy, they really know what I'm going through.*

She opened her eyes, but not to the surprise she was expecting. They had not cleared the room, just a passage through the mess. She looked at them cross-eyed. Then the three fell on the floor, laughing until tears streamed down their faces.

There were other people who helped, relatives and friends. Her parents often cared for her sons. And for six years, Cewe's boss at the restaurant, Dan Alix, overlooked her studying between drink orders. More than once, he worked the bar for her so she could attend her sons' school plays or be home when they were sick.

Co-workers and customers let her know they were amazed at the goal she had set. Some doubted, but others encouraged. Once Cewe had to do a skit for a theater class. As she walked onstage for her monologue, she looked down at the theater seats. Two waitresses were sitting there, a small but precious entourage.

Working at the restaurant was barely enough to cover the bills, let alone pay for college. Cewe took out student loans, and her high class standing helped her win scholarships. When the Wallingford Business and Professional Women's Club first heard about her, they wanted to help. So did many other groups, which gave her $500 here, $200 there, checks that added up to thousands of dollars in tuition that Cewe would not have to repay.

For all those groups she became a cause *célébre*, a symbol of what women who take control of their lives can accomplish. She made the honor society, keeping up a straight-A average for four years.

One hot summer morning in 1989, shortly before she was to start her senior year, Cewe was sleeping in her apartment in Meriden. A silent figure pushed up an unlocked screen and made his way to her bed. The man whispered that if she resisted, he would kill her sons. Then he raped her, dragged her from the apartment, and pushed her into her red Ford Escort.

Twice, he made Cewe pull the car over so he could beat her. Then he forced her into the luggage compartment, where she lay trying to envision escape scenes from movies she had seen. She was certain he would kill her the next time the car stopped. She thought about her sons. It can't be over, she said to herself. *We have so much to look forward to.*

Carefully she unscrewed the pliable cover above her, a thin plastic section that rose when the hatchback was opened. When the car slowed, she picked up the jack, shot through the compartment and slammed the jack against the side of her attacker's head. The car skidded through guardrails and down a 20-foot embankment.

Cewe awoke hours later, her body straddling the front and back seats. Her forehead was split open, and blood was everywhere, matting her hair, covering her clothes. Her attacker was gone.

Her first thoughts were of the boys. What if the man had gone back for them? She stumbled up the rocky ledge to the highway. She had to get to a telephone.

The boys were awakened by their father and the police banging on the apartment's windows. Before answering the door, they went to their mother's room. The bed covers were in a heap and they were afraid she was under them — dead.

For three days, Cewe was at Milford Hospital being treated for injuries to her head and leg and scores of cuts and bruises. She lost sleep knowing her attacker was out there, on the run.

Eventually, Walter Bragdon, the teen-age nephew of Cewe's neighbors, was charged with the attack. According to police, Bragdon had escaped from a prison for minors in Maine, where he had been sent for raping another woman. Weeks after the attack on Cewe, he was captured following a rape in Georgia. He was convicted of that crime, and sentenced to three concurrent life terms and 20 years more.

Six days after Cewe was attacked, her senior year began at Albertus Magnus. Her leg in a brace, her hand bandaged, she drove to class. When she pulled into the parking lot, it was empty. Determined to return, but with her emotions reeling, she had arrived a day early.

The next day, she went back again. Her dream would be her savior. She couldn't let it slip away.

Cewe had planned to take a course to prepare for the law-school entrance exam in December. But now, out of money and emotionally battered, she couldn't do it. Every time she tried to study she had flashbacks. He could have killed her, left her boys motherless — or even murdered them.

The night before the law-school exam Cewe sat at her worn kitchen table. She took a sample test, then worked on a writing exercise. Her thoughts were jumbled. She was terrified. About midnight, she cried herself to sleep. She had worked so hard, overcome so much. The man, "that creep," could take this from her too, if she couldn't force the images from her mind.

Cewe turned the page of the test and took a deep breath. The essay question asked her to make a case for awarding an athletic scholarship to one young woman over another. To the first woman, winning came easily. To the other, success came only through hard work and persistence.

In her essay, Cewe argued the merits of the second woman, the one who wasn't naturally gifted. She was arguing for herself.

Nothing could ease Cewe's anxiety during the eight weeks it took for her test score to arrive. Some of her mail still was being sent to her parents' house, where she had stayed after the rape. The envelope was delivered there one February day in 1990.

Cewe asked her mother to open it while she waited on the telephone. Her mother read every score but the final tally.

"I don't care about that," Cewe said. "Look for the final score!"

At last her mother found it. Above average. Strong enough to get her into law school, though not into the school she wanted.

In the spring, Cewe graduated from Albertus Magnus College magna cum laude. Then she was invited back to her old high school to attend the adult-education graduation. When scholarships were announced, they called her name, again and again. This time the money was for law school. She hustled up to the podium in a cropped jacket and short skirt, frosted blond hair flying. She kept her chin down to hide her tears.

Cewe enrolled in the University of Bridgeport law school. Once, she had dreamed of getting accepted at Yale. That's okay, she says. She'll just teach there someday.

It takes as much courage to have tried and failed as it does to have tried and succeeded.

ANNE MORROW LINDBERGH

WHAT AN AMERICAN GIRL CAN DO

BY

SHERRY BUCHANAN

*L*ois Prater was awakened before dawn by rats scuttling across the wooden floor beneath her iron cot. Sweeping a hand through her soft gray curls, the American missionary rose and began preparing her weekly Bible lessons while it was still relatively cool. The remote Philippine town of Orion would soon be blanketed by suffocating heat and humidity, and the spartan, two-story home of Pastor Olan Quilatan had no tub, shower or air conditioning. *I'll never get used to the weather,* she thought.

Later that muggy morning in 1990 a man and woman dressed in ragged T-shirts and pants came to the door. The woman cradled a baby girl no more than four months old and wrapped in a burlap feed sack.

Prater overheard Pastor Quilatan speaking to the couple in their native Tagalog. "They have six other kids and no job or food," he explained to her. "They ask if the American woman would buy their baby for 1000 pesos (about $40)."

"I'm sorry," Prater stammered, stunned at the offer. Instead she pressed into their hands 300 pesos and a sackful of food. *What will become of that baby?* she wondered, brushing away tears.

Then Prater recalled a promise she had made: "Someday I'll open a home for poor children." But that was the promise of a six-year-old girl, she reminded herself, not a widow of 78.

Missionaries were frequent visitors in the home of Lois's father, Jacob Secrist, a minister in the Assemblies of God church. Many brought stories of a world far removed from the small farms and well-tended apple orchards of Olympia, Wash. None of them made a deeper impression than a pretty, unmarried woman named Lillian Trasher.

Lois, sister Verna and brother Hubert were enthralled by Trasher's stories about Egypt, land of the Pharaohs, and Asyut, a city on the Nile, 250 miles south of Cairo. She also told them about orphaned babies left to die and children left to fend for themselves in narrow, dusty side streets.

On her own in a strange land, Trasher was told again and again it would be impossible to establish an orphanage for these children. The missionary had been harassed by wary villagers, even spat upon. But she persisted and she prevailed.

By the time Trasher visited Olympia to raise funds, her orphanage was seven years old and home to more than 50 children. It was 1918. "An American girl can do anything if she tries hard enough," Trasher told Lois and Verna.

Lois was spellbound by Trasher. For months afterward she and Verna made believe their dolls were orphans, tending them the way they imagined Trasher cared for her children. Six-year-old Lois announced that one day she, too, would have an orphanage.

As a teen-ager, Lois set her sights on mission work. After attending Glad Tidings Bible Institute, she and Verna became co-pastors of a small church in Oregon. But life took an unexpected turn. Verna married and left the pulpit. Then Lois fell in love with a handsome farmhand named Galon Prater, whom she married.

189

The country was mired in the Great Depression, and Galon was lucky to find a construction job. Soon there were three daughters to raise: Barbara, Bonnie and JoAnn. The family moved wherever Galon could find work.

One day in the early 1950s Lois was browsing in a Seattle bookstore when a small biography caught her eye. The title was *The Nile Mother,* and on the green-and-white jacket cover she was startled to see a photograph of Lillian Trasher—now a handsome older woman with graying hair. Prater bought the book and learned that Trasher had since fed, clothed and educated more than 5000 children. *I might have traveled the same road,* Prater mused, and she began to weep.

In the late 1960s Lois and Galon Prater retired to two acres of quiet wooded land in the Lake Stevens district of Washington, 30 miles north of Seattle. There were grandchildren to dote on now, and Lois taught Sunday school. Their comfortable life ended when Galon fell ill with emphysema and died in 1988.

Numb with grief, the 76-year-old Prater was preparing to settle into a new life alone when she happened to see a television interview with a preacher looking for volunteers for a brief mission to Asia. *Do I dare at my age?* she wondered.

Her thoughts turned to Lillian Trasher. *An American girl can do anything if she tries.* Summoning her nerve, Prater called the number and signed on.

But two months before her departure date, Prater suffered a mild heart attack. Soon after, she was back in the hospital a second time, struggling for breath. Now she could only pray.

Several days later Prater's physician entered her room carrying the results of cardiac tests. She dreaded the doctor's verdict, but he wore a look of utter surprise. "I can't find any sign of blockage," he said, shaking his head. "You seem to have the arteries of an 18-year-old."

God has granted me a miracle, Prater thought. She left on the mission in August 1988.

The group preached in Taiwan and Hong Kong, but it was in the Philippines that Prater felt a special tug on her spirit. Tens of thousands of children, many abandoned by destitute or abusive parents, lived on Manila's streets.

There is so much need here, Prater thought, vowing to return. She did so alone in January 1989. For a year she preached in neighborhood churches.

It was on her third trip to the Philippines, in 1990, that the poor couple in Orion tried to sell their baby. From that moment Prater felt a conviction grow within her. Somehow she would start an orphanage.

Back in the United States, her family resisted. "At your age?" her brother Hubert asked. "What if you fall ill again? You can't count on finding a good doctor."

Neighbors were less delicate. "Has your mother gone crazy?" one woman asked daughter Bonnie.

But Lois was determined. In a matter of weeks she sold her house, then held a massive yard sale, watching from the garden as the memories of a lifetime were hauled away. In 1991, with $20,000, she boarded a jet bound for Manila.

Prater searched for a site near Orion. The only one she could afford was about a 12-acre tract of jungle tucked near the foothills of Mount Samat that cost 450,000 pesos ($17,200). It was in an area infested with communist rebels who so far that year had killed several civilians. The provincial commander in Bataan, Col. Enrique Galang, Jr., cautioned her about security.

"I've decided to buy it anyway," Lois replied calmly.

Galang saw the fearlessness in the woman's eyes, then promised to protect her if she would speak to his men about the power of faith. Prater did, and her sessions became a weekly ritual for the soldiers and policemen.

Later Prater returned to the United States on the first of many fund-raising trips. The church groups she spoke to were often wary of funding someone her age, but slowly the gifts added up.

An even tougher chore was taking on the Philippine bureaucracy. Prater would have to register as a corporation with the Securities and Exchange Commission in Manila. That meant a three-hour bus ride in withering heat to the city's outskirts, then another hour wedged into one of the crowded open-air taxis known as jeepneys.

On her first visit a clerk handed her a thick stack of papers to fill out. A second visit elicited the retort that she needed additional addresses. On a third trip a different person said that signatures, which she hadn't obtained, were required. It took more than ten months to get the paper work approved.

Still, her problems were only beginning. She would have to pay 272,324 pesos ($10,400) to hook up electricity—a huge sum. Prater would also need a certified social worker, but the social-welfare agencies told her no one would be willing to relocate to such a remote province. Whenever her frustration verged on despair, she recalled the trials Lillian Trasher had faced.

Therefore, my beloved brethren, be steadfast, immovable, always abounding in the work of the Lord, knowing that in the Lord your labor is not in vain.

1 CORINTHIANS 15

Prater met a contractor, Ed Bacani, who was also a pastor with the Assemblies of God. He looked at the building plans that she had meticulously drawn up herself. *This old lady is willing to sacrifice everything she has to help my people,* he thought. Humbled, he took the job on the spot.

Early each morning Prater walked to the jungle site and with her arthritic hands worked alongside Bacani's men in the stifling heat, stripping away thick vegetation. The workers came to call her affectionately *Lola,* meaning "grandmother." By May 1992 the first stone had been laid.

King's Garden Children's Home was finished in February 1994. The white stucco house had eight bedrooms, a classroom, an American-style kitchen and a laundry—enough room for 30 children. Ed Bacani donated a touch of his own: a floor of beautiful polished stone. A social worker was found.

Finally the day arrived when needy children entered the doors of King's Garden. Alvin, I 1/2 years old, was the first. The child was in desperate straits. His father, accused of a violent crime, was in jail; his mother was close to destitution. When the wispy-haired toddler arrived, he was suffering from untreated bronchitis. But he was soon devouring the home's wholesome food and playing with a roomful of toys.

Alvin was quickly joined by a family of three brothers and a sister: eight-year-old Dandel, six-year-old Budoy, three-year-old David and ten-year-old Marie. Their father, who had been raising them alone, was an abusive alcoholic.

The boys arrived covered with open sores, while the girl had head lice and worms. Quickly they were soaked in a shower, their first ever.

Rose, a I 1/2-year-old with pixie good looks, came next. She cried constantly until a medical examination revealed severe bronchitis. Once that cleared up, she blossomed and was always cheerful.

As word of King's Garden spread, poverty-stricken parents began to arrive, pleading with Lola to take in their children. Within a few months King's Garden had 14 kids ranging in age from nine days to ten years. Prater's daughter Bonnie, a trained nurse, flew over to set up a small dispensary. A doctor in nearby Orion offered free consultations. Many children arrived with spots on their lungs, parasites and intestinal worms. Most were restored to good health.

To Lois Prater, nothing was more rewarding than seeing withdrawn, traumatized children emerge from their shells and begin to grow. Wherever possible, Prater sought to reunite children with their families; otherwise she provided them with the basic necessities and education.

Money was a constant worry because King's Garden depended solely upon private donations. But Prater has a strong faith in God and considerable powers of persuasion. King's Garden was soon home to 33 children, and there are plans for a new dormitory that will hold some 200 more.

Under Prater's care the children have the security of a loving environment and a fixed regimen. There is school in the morning for the older children, and structured play, including a half-hour of singing.

Whenever Lois can break away from fund-raising and endless paper work, she takes the children for long afternoon walks. The youngsters crowd around her, eagerly telling her all about their day. Periodically she loads a group of the kids into the home's van for an excursion.

When night falls, each child is tucked in and read Bible stories. Prater's nights also end with a few quiet minutes studying her Bible. Sometimes just before extinguishing the light, Lois picks up a worn book with a tattered green-and-white cover: her copy of *The Nile Mother.*

Recently at a large family-style dinner, a little boy came up to Prater's side. "I am so happy here," he said. "Now I don't get beat up anymore." Prater enfolded him in her arms and held him close. This, she realized, was the true fulfillment of the dream inspired by Lillian Trasher seven decades ago. With God's help dreams do indeed come true. At any age.

Man never made any material as

resilient as the human spirit.

BERN WILLIAMS

DONALD THORNTON'S
MAGNIFICENT DREAM

BY

JO COUDERT

"What're you lookin' so down in the mouth about, Tass?" Donald Thornton asked his wife. She was feeding their three small daughters when he came home from his meat-packing job, and her eyes met his with an expression he hadn't seen before.

"Didn't you hear?" Tass said softly. "A little girl no bigger than Donna here was raped this afternoon in front of our building."

Donald Thornton now realized what he was seeing in his wife's eyes: the same concern for their daughters' growing up in New York City's Harlem that was worrying him sick. He put his hand on Tass's shoulder. "Start packing," he said. "We're gettin' outa here."

After that evening in 1948, the family moved in with Donald's mother in Long Branch, N.J. Donald got a job digging ditches at nearby Fort Monmouth Army base while Tass worked as a domestic. Soon Donald found a second job delivering home-heating oil at night, and a third on weekends as a bricklayer's helper. The bricklaying job paid only fifty cents an hour, but Donald had a reason for wanting to learn the trade.

196

By the time a fourth daughter, Linda, arrived, Donald had saved enough money to buy a building lot. Deed in hand, he called on the president of the local bank. "Sir," he said quietly, "if you have children you know why I want mine to have a decent place to live." After the men finished talking, Donald Thornton received the first mortgage that the bank had ever granted to a black.

Before starting to build, Donald fenced in the property so the girls could play safely while Tass mixed the mortar and he laid the bricks. Even when she became pregnant again, Tass continued as his hod carrier. "What I need is a boy to help me around here," Donald teased. After baby Rita arrived, Donald took a lot of ribbing about his females. He never knew how to reply until the day he overheard Donna, the oldest, ask Tass what a domestic was.

White kids in Donna's class had been talking about being nurses, pilots and movie stars when they grew up. "I told them I was going to be a teacher," she explained to her mother, "and they said, 'No, you're going to be a domestic.'"

"The next time somebody says that to you," Donald growled, "you tell them you're going to be a doctor." After that, whenever anyone kidded him about what he was going to do with five daughters, he answered, "I'm going to raise doctors."

"Who ya kiddin'?" his friends scoffed. "Your kids'll be having babies by the time they're fifteen just like the rest of the black teen-agers around here."

"Not my girls," Thornton vowed, and he would sit his daughters down around the kitchen table. "Look, kids," he'd say. "I dig ditches for a living. Your ma cleans other people's houses. We don't want that for you. Now, if you're a doctor. . . ."

"But, Dad," they protested. "You got to go to college to be a doctor, and then medical school. Where are we going to get that kind of money?"

"You let your mother and me worry about that," he said. "You just do the studying."

"Studying's your job," Tass echoed, and when one of the girls came home with a less-than-perfect grade, she'd say, "Did anyone in the class get an A? Then you can too. You just have to work harder."

But it wasn't all work, for early on the Thornton sisters had discovered music. At seven, Donna found a toy saxophone in a Cracker Jack box and begged so hard for a real one that her father began asking around. One turned up in somebody's attic, along with a trumpet for Jeanette.

Watching how tirelessly the little girls tried to coax music out of their instruments, Donald made another sacrifice and hired a teacher for them. Later, when Donna switched from alto to tenor sax, Yvonne, the third daughter, pleaded, "Can I learn on Donna's old one?" "You, Cookie?" her father said, laughing. "You're barely big enough to breathe." To prove him wrong, the five-year-old picked up the sax and blew so hard that she fainted.

By the time Yvonne was in second grade, she, Jeanette and Donna were calling themselves The Thornettes and performing for PTA meetings. Soon Linda took up the drums and joined the band.

"I'm thinking maybe I'll try the bass," Donald said to Tass one day. A plan to pay for his daughters' college education was beginning to form in the back of his mind. Try as he might, though, Donald couldn't get the hang of the instrument. He finally turned it over to Tass to learn and got himself a piano. He gave this a good try, too, but soon he was saying to Rita, "Okay, Baby, as soon as your feet can touch the pedals, the piano's for you."

Whenever he had the money, Donald bused his family into New York City, hired a studio and made a practice record so the girls would have the goal of sounding better with each record. "You have to plan five years ahead," he told them. "That way, when I tell you the berries are ripe, the baskets'll be ready for pickin'." The girls didn't need much encouragement. They knew that music would help open the doors of opportunity for them.

In 1960, Donald got the band into an amateur night at Harlem's Apollo Theater. If an act won four weeks in a row, as judged by audience applause, it was hired for a week's appearance on the regular bill. The Thorntons brought the house down, winning in all four appearances. But then the theater changed the rules: "An act has to win six weeks before we book it." Apparently, school kids and their mom in jumpers and tights were not management's idea of a class act.

"Okay, we'll just have to win the next two weeks," Donald told the girls. What he didn't know was that the Apollo would bring in professionals to compete against the band. Even so, the Thorntons' talent, energy and heart rocketed them past the pros.

"They loved us," the youngsters told their father exuberantly. "All we have to do is turn pro and we've got it made."

"Nothin' doing," said Donald. "Music's okay when you're cute kids, but who wants to see a 40-year-old woman blowing her brains out on a horn? When you have one of those things a doctor's got hanging around his neck, you really have something."

The kind of beauty I want most is the hard-to-get kind that comes from within-- strength, courage, dignity.

RUBY DEE

In 1961, teen-ager Betty Jackson, who had been the foster daughter of Donald's mother, joined the Thornton family and came into the band as the sixth sister.

The kids stayed in school, playing locally until 1963, when they accepted an offer to play on a Friday night at Princeton University. Here was a way, Donald realized, for the band to make money without interfering with the girls' schoolwork. He quickly set up a weekend circuit:

Princeton, Friday nights; Yale, Saturday nights; Brown, Sunday afternoons. He bought a van to chauffeur the girls to engagements while they studied in back and Tass worked on costumes. When students volunteered to help them with their electronic equipment, Donald thanked them kindly and said no. "If we stick together and help one another," he said, "there's nothin' this family can't do for itself."

The girls continued to get A's in school. If one had a test, Tass woke her at four in the morning for extra study. "Time is an illusion," she told the girls. "You can always stretch it to make it fit whatever you have to get done."

After graduating from high school, Donna waited a year until Jeanette was finished; then both planned to go to Howard University on

scholarships. "Nothin' doing," their father said. "You're going to college here so we can keep the band together. We have to earn enough to educate all of you."

"But, Daddy," the girls protested, "it's too late to apply here."

"Leave that to me," Donald said. He dressed up in his best suit and called on the president of nearby Monmouth College. When Donald returned home he had special permission for the girls to enter.

As premed students, Donna and Jeanette majored in biology—but then Donna decided that, for all her father's hopes, a career in medicine was not what she really wanted; Jeanette, meanwhile, switched to psychology.

Donald Thornton was crushed. For weeks he scarcely spoke, and when he was home, he did little but sit in his big chair and stare out the window. Then one day, 17-year-old Yvonne sat on the floor beside him and said, "Daddy, I'm going to make it. I'm going to be a doctor. And I'm never going to change my name," she promised. "Even if I marry, I'll always be Dr. Thornton in your honor."

"I believe you, Cookie," he said, and she felt the scrape of his whiskers as he leaned down to hug her.

Yvonne graduated from Monmouth College in 1969, compiling the highest cumulative average of all the biology majors in her class, even though she'd played with the band every weekend of her four years. She was accepted at all 13 medical schools where she applied, finally choosing Columbia University's College of Physicians & Surgeons. She completed her studies in 1973 and became the first black woman to be offered a residency in the department of obstetrics and gynecology at New York City's Roosevelt Hospital.

One day, Yvonne was paged over the hospital's loudspeaker. She found her father at the reception desk, staring at the ceiling. Worried, she took his arm. "What is it, Dad? Has something happened to Mom?"

He turned a rapt face to her. "Did you hear that?" He mimicked the loudspeaker: "'Paging Dr. Thornton. Paging Dr. Yvonne Thornton.' Oh, Cookie, I never heard music as sweet as that."

Looking back later, Donald Thornton felt no disappointment that his dream did not work out precisely as he had planned. After all, he realized, a man's dream should always exceed his reach. And all his daughters had made him proud: Yvonne and Jeanette became doctors (Jeanette also earned a doctorate in psychology before entering medical school, where she became a psychiatrist); Linda became a dentist; Rita is chairman of the science department at a private school and is working toward a doctorate in child development; Betty is a geriatric nurse at a teaching hospital; and Donna became a wife, mother and a court reporter.

All Donald Thornton ever wanted to accomplish, really, was to teach his children what he believed most strongly, the thing that kept him and Tass pushing their family ahead all those years: "If we stick together and help one another, there's nothin' this family can't do for itself."

Far better it is to dare mighty
things, to win glorious triumphs,
even though checkered by failure,
than to take rank with those
poor spirits who neither enjoy
much nor suffer much, because
they live in the gray twilight that
knows not victory nor defeat.

THEODORE ROOSEVELT

THE LITTLEST MARINE

BY

JAY STULLER

On a spring day in 1983, Marine Staff Sgt. Robert Menke was waiting for a hot enlistment prospect he had talked to on the phone. Hunched over paperwork in the Corps' Huntington Beach, Calif., recruiting station, Menke heard the front door open and looked up. In came a boy in a motorized wheelchair, followed by his father. Menke noted the boy's frail body and thin arms. "Can I help you?" he asked.

"Yes," the boy answered firmly. "My name is John Zimmerman."

It took the startled Marine a moment to realize that this was indeed his prospect. "I'm Staff Sergeant Menke," he said, shaking his visitor's small hand. "Come on in."

Menke, a shy man, uncomfortable with recruiting, quickly found himself captured by the articulate, 13-year-old youth with an easy, gap-toothed grin. For more than an hour they spoke—of training and overseas assignments and facing danger. The kid loved the Marine Corps. Not a word was exchanged about the younger Zimmerman's condition or the wheelchair.

There was one basic reason behind the visit to the Marine Corps recruiting office that day. From the moment Richard and Sandra Zimmerman learned their 14-month-old son had Werdnig-Hoffmann syndrome, a rare neurological disease, they vowed to treat him like a normal child.

Told John would probably not live past two, they refused to believe he would die. Despite tremendous weakness in his legs and back and susceptibility to colds, John simply *looked* well.

They had him fitted with a rigid body jacket to help him sit upright and took him on vacation trips all over the country. They didn't get a wheelchair for him until he was three. Even then, Richard Zimmerman often carried his son, who weighed about 30 pounds, lugging him through amusement parks, into restaurants and to movies.

Werdnig-Hoffmann syndrome victims have difficulty fighting off upper respiratory problems. Before the age of five, John was hospitalized three times with pneumonia, each bout putting him on the edge of death. Richard Zimmerman believed that Chicago's cold winter climate was partly to blame, and in 1975 he arranged a job transfer so the family could move to Southern California. There, the boy suffered fewer bouts with respiratory illness.

John, six, was enrolled in classes for orthopedically handicapped children at the Plavan School in Fountain Valley. About this time he became aware of the Marine Corps at a week-long summer camp for disabled children. Many of his counselors at the camp in Cuyamaca Rancho State Park near San Diego were Marine volunteers. Each summer John would get to know another Marine through the camp's one-to-one counseling program. This sparked an interest that evolved into a passion.

While other children worshipped athletic heroes and rock stars, John gathered every bit of material about the Marines he could find. He

I'm a fighter, Mom. A helluva fighter.

plastered his room with Corps recruiting posters, his wheelchair with Marine stickers. His hero was John Wayne. He even dressed like a Marine and, much to his mother's consternation, got a Corps "burr" haircut.

After his initial visit to the Huntington Beach recruiting center, John kept in contact with Menke and Menke's boss, 31-year-old Gunnery Sgt. John Gorsuch. Occasionally he dropped by with his father; more often, he phoned to ask questions or just to talk. He frequently devoted his school reports to Marine tactics, campaigns or equipment.

When new recruiting posters arrived, Menke or Gorsuch would mail or personally deliver one to John. In turn, John built model airplanes, trucks and tanks for his Marine buddies. Though delicate and intricate chores were difficult—and even painful—for him, John would work night after night on the models.

While the Marines inspired John, he gave back as much as he got. One afternoon Gorsuch had scheduled seven appointments for potential recruits. Five hadn't shown up, and the other two had to be disqualified. John called to ask questions for a school report.

"What's wrong, Gunny?" he asked. "You don't sound right." Gorsuch explained. "Ah, come on, Gunny," John said. "Look, you're a smooth operator, and for every one you lose you'll get two more." Gorsuch began to laugh. "You're right Johnny," he said. "You know . . . you're right."

An attempt to move John into a standard fourth-grade class at Plavan failed; because he could not write quickly, he could not keep up. But he made it in the sixth grade after his teachers allowed him to dictate some of his work.

John's family also benefited from his forceful personality. When told something couldn't be done, he would respond, "But did you ask?" Although he realized that he probably never could hold a regular job, he had no fear of talking with strangers and figured that one day he could help his father, a commercial real-estate broker, by making the "cold" calls the elder Zimmerman dreaded.

As close as John was to his Marine friends, he was even closer to his father. Richard Zimmerman helped his son dress in the morning. He helped him with baths and put him to bed each evening.

John rarely talked about the consequences of his disease, but he understood. On a trip to Hawaii in 1982, as the family visited the National Memorial Cemetery of the Pacific, the famed "Punchbowl," John whispered to his father, "I want to be buried here when I die. Can we do it?"

Richard Zimmerman was taken aback. "I don't know if it's possible. But, sure, John. Sure."

In the spring of 1984, not long before John was to graduate from eighth grade, his condition began to worsen. His twisted spine was pressing into his internal organs, pinching nerves that sent searing pain through his back and legs. He had difficulty digesting food, and he began to lose weight. But he was determined to attend graduation.

On the night of the ceremony, John was weak and nauseated, but to his surprise a Marine sergeant was there to escort him. He and the sergeant led the procession of students into the auditorium. John, thin and twisted, had to use the armrest of his wheelchair to prop himself up. His head, normal size, looked much too large for a body that was deserting an able mind. But to a rousing ovation, he flashed his biggest smile.

Then another surprise: it was announced that John was a co-recipient of Plavan's Sergio Duran award, given annually to the handicapped graduate who best overcomes his limitations.

That summer, John's condition improved slightly, and he entered Fountain Valley High School in the fall of 1984. During the first semester, however, his condition began to decline again, and his weight dropped to less than 40 pounds. While he would have preferred to stay home and sleep, he attended school, confiding to his sister that he went "mainly because it makes Mom and Dad happy."

On New Year's Eve, John went into respiratory failure and was rushed to the hospital.

Gorsuch and Menke visited daily. Realizing that their 15-year-old friend's remaining days would be few, they set out to make him a Marine. Menke secured permission to name John an honorary member of the Corps. Then one of Menke's friends penned a one-of-a-kind proclamation. On January 15, in a hospital room crowded with family and Marines, Maj. Robert Robichaud, area recruiting director, read the document. "By reposing special trust and confidence in the fidelity and abilities of John Zimmerman, I do hereby appoint him an Honorary Marine . . ."

Two days later John looked at Sandra and said, "I'm a fighter, Mom. A helluva fighter." That night, he spoke to his nurses about dying, saying that his only fear was how his parents and sister would fare without him. In the early hours of January 18, John Zimmerman, U.S. Marine, passed on.

In a eulogy at John's memorial service, Gorsuch, his voice cracking, said, "Marines learn never to give up, and John definitely had that quality. We have a motto in the Marines, the Latin words for always faithful. This is for Johnny Zimmerman," he concluded. *"Semper fi."*

After the service, the two Marines approached John's casket. Slowly, Menke and Gorsuch unpinned the Marine emblems from their coat collars and gently placed these symbols of fidelity into the casket with their friend.

During the final week of his life, no longer able to talk, John had scrawled a note to his father, reminding him of a promise made nearly three years before. "Punchbowl—will you visit me?" His father nodded. "If that's what you want, we'll do it," he said.

In reality, Richard had no idea if it would even be possible. Yet his son's favorite phrase kept coming back to him: "But Dad, did you ask?"

Richard looked into the matter and discovered that such cemeteries are reserved for military personnel and their families. Even though Menke had volunteered to give up his cemetery plot, the Veterans Administration would not permit it, or grant John's wish. Richard decided to try again. This time he wrote to California Senator Pete Wilson and learned that to circumvent the rules he would need authorization from the President. The Senator, a former Marine, was willing to help.

"He never had the opportunity to serve his country in the Marine Corps as he so wished he could have," Wilson wrote to President Reagan. "However, his dedication and courage no doubt had very positive effects on many young Marines and civilians . . ."

The President granted the request, and the Marine Corps went into action. At Camp Smith on Oahu, about 30 Marines volunteered for the funeral detail. And on a windy day in the Punchbowl, with the cemetery's flag at half-staff, John Zimmerman was put to rest with full military honors.

Prior to a 21-gun salute, U.S. Navy Chaplain Jack Graham spoke. "Courage isn't limited to battlefields," he said. "The Marine Corps has a saying: 'The Marines need a few good men.' They found one in John Zimmerman."

It is curious that physical courage should be so common in the world and moral courage so rare.

MARK TWAIN

THE
SEASON STARTS
TOMORROW

BY

KATIE McCABE

is nose pressed against the window, Terrence Thomas squint-ed into the late-afternoon sunlight and scanned the traffic whizzing past St. Jude High School. He tensed as yet another car slowed at the traffic light out front, sure this was the one bringing the coach he and his teammates had been awaiting for hours—or months, or years, depending on how you counted.

"Hey y'all," he said. "Check this out."

On his left, six-foot-three-inch Damon Childrey crouched lower, while the other seniors, Darin Irwin and Amir Green, jostled to get a look at the sleek white van easing across traffic. It slowed at the stone pillars and glided into the circular driveway, its green-tinted windows glinting in the sunshine.

"It's headin' for the gym," said Terrence's friend Horace Lewis. "Maybe it's him, Tee."

"Maybe it ain't," Terrence shot back.

"Maybe y'all don't know *who* it is!" someone else snorted.

At that, the group lapsed into silence. How often they had talked, in the blistering heat of the Alabama summer, of the season that was upon them, of the state championship they'd dreamed about since the five of them had first shot hoops together—Terrence and Horace and their older buddies, Damon and Darin and Amir.

On those endless, sultry evenings, they sat in the dark on Terrence's front stoop and talked basketball. Their old coach had been just fine, their 14-12 record passable. But with a new coach, '93 could—*would*—be the season the St. Jude Pirates finally made liars of the tall Montgomery public-school guys who laughed at the "little Catholic boys."

In July and August, it was all so easy to believe. But now it was October—October 15 to be exact, with varsity tryouts scheduled for 5 p.m.—and still no word on a new coach. The boys had gathered in the school foyer the moment the dismissal bell rang, and were hunched at the window, trying to make out the driver as the van slowed to a stop by the gym. The four letters on the license plate came into view. "W-A-L-T," they read.

No one moved, their eyes fixed on the driver's door. But it remained closed. Instead, the passenger side flew open. A man's head and shoulders appeared, and a blue-carpeted ramp flipped out. Then they saw it.

"*The guy is in a wheelchair,*" someone whispered. "Our new basketball coach is in a wheelchair."

"No, he's not," Terrence protested. " 'Cause that's not the coach!"

"Who else'd be pullin' up to the gym at five o'clock? That's him."

"You're lying," Terrence fired back. "I'm goin' to ask Mrs. Perry." He shot into the main office. The others followed and met principal Geraldine Perry coming out, smiling. They relaxed a little when they saw her. *Surely,* they thought, *Mrs. Perry had more sense than to hire a coach who couldn't walk.* She was such a huge basketball fan she went to away games even their mothers missed.

"It's not true, is it?" Terrence asked. "About that guy in the wheel-chair bein' our new coach?"

"It certainly is," she told them.

The boys stood staring at her. Why would she do something to embarrass the Pirates all over the city?

"His name is Mr. Walt Kennedy, and you all are lucky to have some-one like him to learn from. Let's go welcome him," she said, setting off down the hallway.

The man who'd just arrived, she explained as the boys loped along beside her in stunned silence, had been a college basketball legend—at *her* college, Florida A&M. After that he was a Harlem Globetrotter, then the coach of superstar high-school teams in Washington, D.C. And yes, she said, he did have a disability—multiple sclerosis had put him in a wheelchair a few years ago. "Which of course has nothing to do with anything," Mrs. Perry finished, throwing open the double doors that led outside to the gym.

Walter Kennedy was handsome, and gray-bearded, and big. Everything about him seemed oversized—the broad, muscled shoulders and neck, the long legs and enormous feet of an exceptionally tall man. Rapidly he rolled along the length of the van, pressing buttons, sliding the doors into place.

The boys hung back, and then, seeing Kennedy reach for the rope to hoist up the ramp, they moved forward, relieved to have something to do to fill the awkward silence.

Damon was the first to find his voice. "Need a hand, sir?" he asked.

Kennedy paused, and Damon shifted uncertainly as he felt the new coach's serious brown eyes rest on him. When Kennedy spoke, his voice was not unfriendly, but something in his tone—something iron, Damon thought—made the boys step back.

"No, son," Kennedy said. "I can handle it."

In the gym, they fell into line without a word, studying Kennedy as he buzzed in his chair around the court, calling the boys to order in a deep, steady voice that echoed off the walls.

He was cool and all business, Terrence thought. And quiet. Terrence looked sideways at Horace and Amir. They were looking straight ahead, waiting, as he was, for this no-nonsense man who had introduced himself as "Coach Kennedy" to say something besides his name—something that would tell them what he was all about.

Instead, there was the sound of the whistle, followed by curt, clear directions for running scrimmages. Then layup, ball-handling and running drills followed. All that long evening, and the next, and the next, the boys tried to read this man.

As they filed in the following Monday, his varsity picks, taped to the gym door, told them something about what lay behind the coach's silent scrutiny during the tryouts. The real superstars were listed, of course—Darin, the stocky, agile shooter who had more or less carried the team in previous seasons; Damon, with his height and golden hands; Terrence and Horace, who'd started on varsity as underclassmen. But other varsity veterans who hadn't bothered to hustle for the new coach found they'd lost their spots to junior varsity, or JV, players who had—even five-foot-four-inch Amir, who'd just about given up making the team because of his height.

Kennedy waited for the disappointed few to file out, then began speaking. "The first thing I want to say to you all is that I didn't come here just to do a little bit better than last season." Boys who'd been whispering, discussing the cuts, stopped talking. "I came here to win it all. We're going to Birmingham."

Terrence's cheeks burned. *Birmingham. State finals.* He and the other guys had talked about these goals all summer long. But a *coach*—even one who'd been a Globetrotter—coming out with a statement that brazen on the first day of practice, before he'd even seen them play? How on earth,

Terrence wondered, was he going to do this? Show them Globetrotter moves? From a wheelchair?

"Things are going to be a lot different with me in charge," Kennedy continued, buzzing back and forth in front of the bleachers, meeting each boy's eyes for a moment or two. "The first thing is, I hold team meetings before each practice." Murmurs of annoyance rippled through the row of boys sitting on the bleachers.

"Report to the cafeteria, not the gym. And be on time," Kennedy continued, his low voice cutting through the grumbling. "Players who are not on time will be suspended. So will players who fail to come fully dressed in uniform."

From the far end of the line came a muffled exclamation of disgust. Kennedy stopped short. "I hear y'all makin' those noises," he said. "You might as well know right now, I run things my way. I'm here to do a job. I'm not here to be anybody's friend."

Terrence didn't have to look at his buddies to know they were thinking the same thing he was: who'd *want* to be friends with this guy? Compared to their old coach's easygoing style, Kennedy's intensity grated on them. None of the new regimen made sense to them: the team meetings, the rules, the endless drills. He started that afternoon and kept hammering into them day in, day out.

"Again! Till you get it right!" came the voice from the far side of the gym as a dozen pairs of sneakers squeaked to a halt. "Y'all think the coach isn't watchin'?" Kennedy taunted them. "Coach sees everything!"

That was the worst of it. He did. The wheelchair didn't slow him down a bit; in fact, it seemed to give him an edge. He rolled the length of the gym, driving home the pitfalls of zone defense—guarding areas of the court instead of individual opponents in a man-to-man defense. He pounced on every ragged drive, every missed rebound, every sloppy pass.

Players like Darin and Damon, who'd been untouchable in the old regime, took their lickings right along with everyone else. When

Kennedy slapped them with extra drills, they bit their lips, knowing that if they didn't want to warm the bench in the season opener, they'd better keep their mouths shut. Every night from five o'clock to seven, they followed Kennedy's commands, training their eyes on the floor lest he see their fury.

"Practice ain't no fun anymore," Amir told Terrence and Horace one night as they trudged home, sweating and shivering in the autumn darkness. The two juniors looked at each other, wondering what to say to Amir, who had been working his heart out for the coach. They had another shot next year. But for Amir and the other seniors, this was it.

"It's different all right," Terrence snorted. "He wears us down so bad with drills we fall apart in scrimmage. Then he rips us up. Seems like he's just waiting to tear us apart."

Horace kicked at the gravel and let out a sigh. The coach had made him team captain, so naturally the other guys thought he knew something about Kennedy they didn't. The truth was he had no more idea what was going on than they did.

"Forget trying to figure him out, y'all," he said finally. "Season starts in another week. We got so much talent on this team, we're gonna tear 'em up, coach or no coach. What difference does it make what he says, long as we win?"

Opening night of the season. They were pumped to get their hands on the ball and wow the crowd that had turned out to see them whip Loachapoka.

In the hallway, Kennedy fired a volley of last-minute instructions. "Stay on your man, ya' hear, just stay on your man till the very end," he intoned, ticking off the pitfalls of zone defense for what seemed to Terrence like the dozenth time. He tuned out Kennedy's voice as he huddled with his teammates and piled his hand atop theirs.

"What TIME is it?" Terrence yelled.

"IT'S . . . SHOW TIME!" they yelled back, charging onto the court.

The whistle blew, and the anger, the exhaustion, the frustration of the last four weeks dissolved in the roar of the crowd, and there was only motion, and grace, and speed.

The ball was in Terrence's hands and he scanned the court, picking his path, dodging and weaving, untouchable on his way to the basket. Again and again he penetrated and scored.

He was hot, and so were his teammates—Darin was making long three-point baskets from the outside; Amir turned into a spitfire on the court; Horace was yelling instructions and sinking baskets. All of them eased into zone defense when they tired of man-to-man; but they eased past Loachapoka too.

When the final buzzer sounded, they fell on one another hooting and hollering. They'd won, 61-48, and they'd done it *their way.*

The next Monday, as they strolled down the hall to practice, Horace told the others, "It's paying off, all that time we spent playin' together in the summertime."

"All our *lives,* man," laughed Darin, remembering the grade-school teams they'd started on years ago. "Coach has gotta see the chemistry."

"Yeah, and stop tryin' to mess with it," Terrence said, not bothering to lower his voice as he turned the corner toward the cafeteria. "I mean, we *punished* those guys . . ."

When he saw Kennedy, he broke off. The coach was waiting quietly, wearing an expression Terrence couldn't quite read. Not disgusted, exactly. Just unimpressed. Kennedy waited until the last backpack had thudded to the floor and then he began talking.

"The season," he said, "starts tomorrow."

The boys sank onto the cafeteria benches, bewildered. This man talked in riddles. *Tomorrow?* They'd just crushed Loachapoka, and he wanted to say they hadn't even begun yet?

"*Tomorrow,* you all are going to start playing like a well-disciplined ball team. I don't want raggedy ballplayers. I want tough ballplayers, and that means one thing—tough defense. I saw Horace putting you all in zone when you got tired."

Terrence stared straight ahead, following the minute hand of the cafeteria clock as it marked the next 20 minutes. As Kennedy droned on, Terrence ignored him. In a few days there'd be the sound of another whistle, the beginning of the magic once again, the time when nothing mattered but the joy of playing, and with any luck at all, they'd have another victory.

Terrence might have been able to ignore Kennedy forever if the coach hadn't had the gall—after several big victories—to call an extra practice on a Saturday.

Arriving at the gym that morning, Terrence was annoyed—not enough to skip practice altogether but enough to take his time getting there. On a weekend, surely, even a fanatic like Kennedy wouldn't be clock-watching.

A teammate met him at the gym door. "You're in big trouble, Tee," he whispered. "Coach just got on my case for being a couple of minutes late, and he's been asking every few minutes, 'Where's Terrence?' "

"Okay, I'm here now, man," Terrence answered impatiently. *So Coach was waiting for me,* he thought. He'd been waiting too—waiting for Kennedy to say something about how he blasted into the season opener by putting 14 points on the board—something like 'Good game' or even 'Not bad.' No matter how hard he hustled, though, there was nothing but criticism. His cheeks burning, he dribbled his way down court to where the coach was buzzing back and forth between two lines of players.

For once, Kennedy didn't have to blow his whistle to halt practice. All he did was swing his wheelchair around to face Terrence, and the dribbling stopped.

"Team, what time did I say practice started?"

"Nine o'clock," they answered in unison.

Kennedy slowly extended his left arm straight out so that the face of his big wristwatch was at Terrence's eye level.

"Terrence, what time is it now?"

Terrence felt his teammates' eyes on him and he shrugged. "You're the one with the watch," he told the coach. "You tell me."

The other boys laughed uneasily. Kennedy's voice didn't change, but his face did. "Out," he said. Terrence stood stock-still, looking at him. "Get your things and go home."

Terrence surprised himself, his answer came so quickly.

"No," he told Kennedy. Once he spoke, he found he couldn't stop. "I got up this morning and I came all the way up here. I'm not going home …"

But Kennedy had already turned away. "Come on, team," he said to the other players. "Let's move to the other side of the gym."

For a moment, no one even breathed. The boys gazed in silence at their friend as he walked over to the bleachers and sat, and at Coach Kennedy.

Damon studied the coach's face, now calm and businesslike. There was not a trace of the look that had flashed across it a moment ago. But Damon couldn't forget it. What he'd seen was anger, deep anger, and it frightened him.

Slowly, Damon moved across the gym, and the others moved with him. They began passing and shooting, but their minds were on Terrence—out for good, they figured, unless he apologized.

Horace, who never lost his cool, kept muddling the drills; Darin, always quiet, grew even quieter. And Amir kept sneaking glances at Terrence sitting, chin in hands, his eyes following the players. Up until this year, Amir had warmed the bench himself. He knew there was nothing worse than having to sit and watch other people doing the thing you loved best. But Terrence shouldn't have talked the way he did to the coach; Amir knew that. They all did.

And it was getting plainer by the minute to Terrence. When nearly two hours had passed, he was still on the outside, looking in. He'd known it was wrong as soon as the words were out of his mouth. Now he had to find a way to apologize to Kennedy before he lost his chance to play basketball for good.

Kennedy's whistle blew to end practice and Terrence stood up. He began walking, then running, after the coach, who was whizzing toward the athletic office to lock up.

"Coach," he said, his heart pounding. Kennedy kept moving.

"Coach," he called out, "I'd like to talk to you for a minute." Kennedy stopped and looked around, his face impassive. Terrence's mouth went dry.

"I want to apologize, Coach," he said, struggling. "I'm sorry about the way I talked."

There. At least it was out. Whatever the coach said to him now, he knew he had it coming.

"You know something, Terrence?" Kennedy said slowly, deliberately. "You're a good ballplayer. A very good ballplayer." He paused, but Terrence was too stunned to say anything. Then Kennedy leaned forward, his face more serious than Terrence had ever seen it. "But the one thing I want you to remember," he added, "is that on my ball team, people respect each other."

With that, he turned his wheelchair, pulled out the keys to his office and began rolling rapidly away.

220

In the parking lot, Terrence's teammates were huddled, waiting for him.

"Yeah, yeah, Coach and I had a good talk, we got it straight," he said, assuring his friends that he was still on the team.

They didn't tell Terrence how scared they'd been at the dead-calm way Kennedy had moved them across the gym floor, silently pulling the team apart.

Here was a man who had his eye on a state championship, and yet he would have booted a top scorer and risked throwing the rest of the team into chaos. It took their breath away. *He* took their breath away, with the price he put on respect.

And yet, they still didn't have his respect, and there seemed to be no way to get it. Every other coach they'd known would have been hollering his lungs out to see the way they were trashing their opponents. Twice they drove the score over 100 while keeping the other teams below 70. They even edged past tough Calhoun High by a single point.

For days after that victory—their fifth with no losses—they were heroes around school. Mrs. Perry praised the varsity over the intercom; the JV players clustered around them, high-fiving them on their way into practice. Girls who'd never noticed them before were lingering by their lockers wanting to talk basketball.

But Kennedy just told them they couldn't take credit for the talent God gave them. Talent alone, he said over and over, never got anybody through the bad times.

Nobody could quite make out just what made a guy a "real ballplayer" in Kennedy's eyes. "You can't see your weaknesses when you're winning," he warned, as grim-faced as if they had zero wins and five losses, instead of the other way around.

Much as they wanted to, they couldn't shrug that off, not from someone who watched ballplaying the way Coach Kennedy did. He had a "court vision" he trained on their opponents, and would rattle off details about weaknesses and strengths most coaches wouldn't see.

So when he dissected *them* from that rolling throne of his, it was tough to argue. "I want you boys to tell me," he'd begin quietly, each time they fell out of man-to-man, "how you expect to keep winning when you got no defense?"

"But Coach," Horace tried to tell him once, "we *got* a defense. We're winning games with it."

Kennedy's eyebrows shot up, and Horace stopped. "You know something?" Kennedy sighed, closing his eyes and shaking his head. "You boys are hardheaded. Real hardheaded. Don't you know that zone is banned in the NBA? *It is not for real ballplayers.* How many times do I have to tell you all: man-to-man is the best defense. A guy gets past you in man-to-man, it's your fault. Nobody else's. There's always gonna be knuckleheads saying zone is easier. Sure it's easier. But that doesn't make it right."

Terrence and Horace glanced at each other, knowing Kennedy would never budge on that one. In his book, guys who didn't carry their own weight in defense weren't just bad ballplayers. They were no-account buck-passers, and he had no use for them.

There was a time when they'd known as clearly as their own names the truths of basketball: that talent really did see a player through; that great ballplaying came from inside the man, and that winning was all that really counted in the end.

But Kennedy, with his silent messages about respect mattering more than championships, with his tirades and his taunts, his endless drilling and ironclad rules, had managed to shoot the air out of all of it. In a few weeks' time, he'd taken away everything. All they had to hang on to was one another.

Then, in one horrible, humiliating weekend, Coach Kennedy took that away too.

He did it when it counted most, right in the middle of their big Christmas Tournament, in front of a standing-room-only holiday crowd and a slew of reporters who'd come to see the Pirates grab their division's No. 1 spot.

At first it looked like an ordinary substitution when Coach Kennedy raised his hand in the first game and sent in Sidney Robbins, a player he'd just pulled up from the JV. But when he *started* the second game with Sidney instead of Amir, it was as though he'd hauled off and whacked everybody on the team. It was one thing, they mumbled in the locker room, to substitute one veteran for another; it was downright insulting to send in some rookie. And they ended up losing both games.

They burned as they looked at Sidney sitting in the team meeting the Monday after the double loss. A few players were already so furious before the second game they hadn't even bothered to warm up as required. They'd just plopped onto the bench, aware of nothing but the boos from the bleachers and the coach's impassive face as the St. Jude crowd yelled, "Put Amir in!"

Now Kennedy had on a blank look as he rolled into the gym. He began calling out the names of the players who'd defied him by sitting out their warm-ups on the bench.

"You four who skipped," he said, "are suspended for two games. Out." Once the door closed behind the four boys, he turned to the smaller group that remained behind. "All right," he said, "let's talk about the other problem."

What a way to refer to the weekend's fiasco, Terrence fumed, replaying in his mind the way they'd collapsed the minute the coach sent in Sidney.

Softly, almost soothingly, Kennedy began speaking about moving on, putting your losses behind you, winning the next one—things, Terrence suddenly realized, that *normal* coaches, coaches with real hearts, said to their teams all the time. Except that Kennedy didn't have a heart. He had a lot of nerve, urging them to move on like men, after he'd sabotaged them.

"Tell me," Kennedy asked, "what do you all think about what happened?"

Until that moment, Terrence hadn't realized how much he had hated—*really hated*—this season, every stinking bit of it, starting with Kennedy's ridiculous boast that they were going to Birmingham, to his monotonous drills and post-game harangues, and now to booting a third of the team.

Terrence sat speechless and so did everybody else, until at last Amir raised his hand.

"Coach, I really don't think you've been giving me enough credit for what I've done for the team," Amir said, fighting to control the anger in his voice. "I've been on this team from Day One, giving it all I got, and then when it comes to the tournament, you start Sidney instead of me. That's not fair."

Terrence was sure Kennedy would tear into Amir and tell the rest of them they were amateurs for unraveling at the kind of substitution NBA coaches made every day. But as he studied Kennedy's face, he saw that this was going to be different.

"All right," the coach was urging the team, "now we're getting to the meat. Say what's on your mind. Get it out."

It was as though he'd opened a dam. "I don't think it was fair either," Damon said, and then Darin and Horace jumped in. Kennedy kept calling on people, listening, until finally everybody except Terrence had spoken.

"Terrence," Kennedy asked, "what do you have to say?"

Terrence's mind churned. There was so much more tugging at him than the Sidney business, or even the two losses. "I agree with the other guys, Coach," he said finally. "I really don't have anything to add."

Kennedy's eyes swept the line. Then he started talking about coaches, about how, sometimes, they saw things in players that the other players just couldn't see. "I pulled up Sidney from the junior varsity because I think he brings something to the team that no one else has. That's the ability to play real tough, aggressive defense, to agitate the ballhandler. I'm looking for the very best combination of players for this team, *and I'm going to keep experimenting until I find it,*" he said, closing the case on Sidney and Amir the way he closed every case, Terrence thought—on his side of the argument. He'd opened up for a moment, but that moment was over now and the old Kennedy was back.

"I'm the coach. This is my team. I run it the way I see fit. You may not always agree with my decisions, but you're going to have to abide by 'em. You got two choices: you can either suck it up, play hard, fight for your spot—or you can be a quitter. It's my way or the highway. On my team, there's no in between."

Nobody said a word to Coach Kennedy, and for the rest of that long, empty New Year's weekend, everybody just went home and kept quiet. When their diminished team came trailing back to school the Tuesday after vacation, they still weren't talking.

"There's no in between," the coach had said of fighting and quitting. But there was. There was a whole gray world in the middle, and they were in it. People walked into the locker room that morning with their uniforms for the away game, avoided each other's glances, and banged locker doors shut without a word.

Horace wasn't there. All through first period, and second, and third, Terrence waited, watching the parking lot. Finally, by lunchtime, it was obvious Horace wasn't going to show. He hadn't said anything about being sick the night before, when they'd talked on the phone. That meant that the team captain, the coach's main man, the guy who was supposed to keep everyone else on track, had skipped school on a game day.

The look that crossed the coach's face when he called Horace's name at game time was one Terrence had never seen before. Kennedy was worried. The look persisted as Kennedy asked about Horace again and again.

"It's like we told you, Coach," Terrence said. "He wasn't in school today. He must be sick."

The locker room echoed with the sound of Amir's voice as he led the team in the prayer they said before all their games. And then it was Show Time, and what little was left of the starting lineup trotted out to take on a team they bragged they could trash on their worst day.

With no backup team, this *was* their worst day. Somehow, though, as they were playing basketball, the little bit of pride they had left welled up inside them, pulling them through until they racked up 74 points to their opponents' 60. That wasn't exactly a "trashing," but it still beat losing, especially with only half a team and no captain.

"What happened, man?" Terrence asked Horace late that night on the phone. "Coach was asking for you 'bout a hundred times. I think he knew you weren't really sick."

Horace's voice was flat and empty. "Well, I was sick," he said, "sick of playing basketball. I don't care if I play another game this year. I really don't."

"You do too," Terrence said, panicking. It was one thing to run off at the mouth himself. It was another to hear a guy like Horace talk about quitting.

"Horace."

"Yeah."

"How long we been playing basketball? How long we been *loving* basketball?"

"I know, Tee, I know. But it's not the same."

"That's what you think *today*. But you're gonna wake up tomorrow wishing you could play. And you won't be able to." Horace didn't say a word, and Terrence knew he'd hit home. "Think about it: life without basketball," he said. "If you don't play for him, you don't play at all. Then he wins."

It was enough to get Horace back to practice. The suspended players also returned but, like everybody else, they felt they were marking time. In the six months since those magical, steamy summer nights on Terrence's front stoop, their championship dream had faded into a blur of drills and endless work and humiliation.

But as they headed into the big Martin Luther King, Jr., Tournament in mid-January, the coach began teasing and coaxing and even praising them. He pulled Amir out during practice for private talks. And he yanked the rest of the guys out of the shadows with some of the same stories that had infuriated them since the day he came.

"Frank," he'd say—or Amir or Terrence, or whoever had thrown the last sloppy pass—"you know who you remind me of? John Battle." The first time he told the story, the gym went quiet; everybody was so amazed to hear the coach comparing one of them to an NBA player who was a guard for the Cleveland Cavaliers.

"I coached John Battle in Washington, D.C., when he was in high school," he continued, pausing and leaning backward as they digested that incredible piece of information. "When I first got hold of that boy—before I started teaching him things and he started listening—he was just like you. A knucklehead."

They'd gotten used to the knucklehead zing, though it always stung. But now, every once in a while, in the middle of the taunts and the sermons, the coach threw in a story of another knucklehead, a boy from Tuskegee who got a licking for shooting hoops when he should have been working. His name was Walt Kennedy.

"I got the whipping of my life once for bein' lazy, like you boys," he told them, as if getting a licking was the greatest thing that could happen to a kid. "I was always looking for a way to play basketball, even when I was supposed to be doin' something else."

None of them could imagine a time far enough in the past for Coach Kennedy to have been a kid, let alone a kid who was crazy about basketball. But he was.

In fact, a long story about him in their local newspaper had made a big deal about how much he loved the sport, about his 23-year battle with multiple sclerosis, and how he'd refused to let it drive him from basketball. For ten years after his diagnosis, according to the article, he'd kept right on coaching his McKinley Tech team in Washington, D.C., until finally, in 1980, it seemed there was no way to continue and he retired. But when he returned to his boyhood home in Tuskegee, he grew hungry for coaching, hungry, he explained, to help more players go to college through basketball. In the fall of '91, he took a coaching job at a Tuskegee high school.

And then came a second blow. Getting ready to drive to a game one day, he was hoisting himself into the driver's seat and he fell. In the three hours before someone found him, he had made up his mind to quit coaching for good. But after a few days away from basketball, he knew he couldn't live without it. Disability or no, Kennedy decided to come back, and when he heard of an opening at St. Jude's two years later, he telephoned Mrs. Perry.

Everything about it made sense when they read the newspaper story, and yet, none of it did. The man who called them knuckleheads and pounded on them till their heads ached seemed a different person from the newspaper hero with his quiet quotes about wanting to give something of himself to another group of boys.

But even they had to admit they got a glimpse of that man when they listened to the coach tell about skipping his chores as a boy to shoot hoops. If ever a kid loved basketball, it was the Walt Kennedy in his story.

"One day, my daddy asked me to mow the lawn, and I said, 'Sure, I'll get to it.' Then I ran up to the church parking lot to shoot hoops," he told them, laughing. "He came home at lunch, asked me again, and I told him I would. But I didn't. I went to play ball. Well, when he got home that evening, he didn't say a word. He just walked out back to the woods and cut down the biggest switch you ever saw."

By this time Kennedy was laughing so hard he could barely tell the story. "And he gave me a whipping I never forgot! I want to tell you boys something. My daddy was a tough man. He was a tough man!"

Incredibly, after the nightmare of the Christmas Tournament, after having their team torn apart, they were all still playing basketball and winning. Just how they'd made it this far—9-2 heading into the big January tournament—nobody was quite sure. But there was no doubt about how they were going to get the rest of the way: by Kennedy's rules, or not at all.

In those days nobody made it through one hour of practice without feeling the yank of his iron chain. People caught lagging got dragged out front and center with a loud "You want to pout? Go home." He drilled into even the youngest, most inexperienced guys the understanding that the road to state finals wasn't just long. It was hard. Once you made it through your area tournament, you were up against some of the toughest teams in Alabama.

For a private-school ballclub like St. Jude's, in the division of the state's smallest schools, that was going to be a big jump. "You ain't even close to tough," Kennedy had told them way back in October. And those autumn practices began to look easy compared to his January routine:

push-ups till they dropped; calisthenics to tighten muscles they never knew they had; extra laps for falling out of man-to-man into zone. It would have been completely unbearable except that somehow, so slowly they couldn't say when it happened, they realized it was making a difference.

The fans didn't see it, but everybody on the team could sense the improvement: the extra minute or two or three that they managed to last in man-to-man; the second wind that let them hold down the score against strong teams. It felt good, that rush of power, that bit of breathing room.

It would have felt better, of course, if Coach Kennedy had let them pause to savor it a little. "That's over, that's past you," he told them as they pulled past tall, tough Montgomery County High not just once but twice. "The season starts tomorrow." Tomorrow, he said, they'd all stay in man-to-man through the final quarter. Tomorrow, every guy would hold his own on defense.

"The only way you're gonna go all the way," he repeated until they heard it in their sleep, "is to be your own coach on the court, talkin' to each other play by play. You gotta hone your defense so airtight nobody can get through. There is only one kind of defense that is airtight. What kind is that, team?"

"Man-to-man, Coach," they answered in chorus.

"What kind?" he'd thunder, cupping a hand against his ear.

"Man-to-man!"

"Again! Louder!"

"Man-to-man!"

There was no escaping the chant, Terrence thought, any more than you could escape Kennedy himself. Kennedy wanted them to play basketball his way: never giving the other guy room to breathe; standing your ground at any price; pounding away like a jackhammer till the opponent finally folded.

They were pushing, all of them. They ran such a tight defense against Alabama Christian that the opponent's coach told the newspapers, "We walked into a buzz saw." When the whistle blew to begin the second match against Calhoun, it was Kennedy's chants setting them in motion, Kennedy's instructions running them through the plays, Kennedy's drills echoing in their heads so clearly they almost forgot how unreadable the coach's expressionless face looked to the people in the stands.

"Doesn't that man *ever* get excited?" Terrence's mother asked him after she watched them rack up a series of wins that put the regional tournament within reach.

Terrence shook his head. "We're going to Birmingham, Mom. Coach can't be fooling around, yelling and acting crazy. He's got bigger things on his mind."

It would have been nice, every once in a while, to hear Kennedy holler so the fans would know he thought his team did a few things right. And yet, Terrence thought, Kennedy had ways of showing them when they'd pleased him—funny, backhanded little pats the fans couldn't see. And he remembered the first time Kennedy gave him a compliment wrapped in one of his insults. Terrence's head was pounding so hard with exhaustion after a two-hour defense drill he barely heard the coach calling him over.

"Terrence."

"Yes, sir?"

"You had a good practice tonight, didn't you?"

"It sure felt like it to me," he said, flushing with pleasure.

"You're a knucklehead, boy, you know that, don't you?" Kennedy's grin was so big as he spoke that before Terrence knew it, he was grinning back.

"You're a knucklehead," the coach repeated. "But I gotta play you. After a practice like that, I gotta play you."

And in those moments when Kennedy shook his head in awe at a play executed to perfection, his face shining with admiration, they saw the boy he told of in his whipping story, and the man they'd read about in the paper—a man who loved basketball. He loved it so much, the article said, that when he'd come to St. Jude's, he had agreed to coach their team for free.

Kennedy never said a word to them about that, and if Mrs. Perry hadn't mentioned it to a local reporter, they would never have known. The money meant nothing to him, the way the paper reported the story; it was the satisfaction he wanted.

That made sense, except that Kennedy taught at a high school near his home in Tuskegee, which meant that every day after work he drove an hour each way to run practice at St. Jude's.

He'd told the boys about the drive one afternoon after he first came, but they hadn't given it another thought. Kennedy never talked about it again.

It was only at those moments in practice when the coach beamed so much his face shone that the boys thought about who he was, where he'd been. Back in the early 1960s, before he started coaching, Kennedy had been one of those players who'd mastered basketball so completely he could dance through it. For three years he'd traveled the world, not just playing, but performing. It seemed far away and long ago to them, all that Globetrotter magic, and yet when they executed a maneuver with grace and speed and precision, for that split second in time, they felt they were part of that.

Those moments didn't come often, but they lasted. You could go a long, long time in the glow of one of those looks, sit through a lot of harangues. And that was what the coach was doing more and more as January rolled into February and they began their "countdown to Birmingham."

More and more they were asked the question that had shocked them when he first asked it: "What do you think?" Sometimes, it was hard to say what they thought in front of everybody else, to say they lost to Loachapoka the first weekend in February because Horace and Terrence had shut out Darin a little, because Damon had fouled too many times, because they'd let a few too many of the opponents' men penetrate the defense.

It was funny, Terrence thought, that a man so bent on taking them to state finals would not be obsessed with winning and losing. When they prayed as a team before games, they asked only for good sportsmanship and no injuries. And when they fell to Alabama Christian just a week after they'd beaten them 94-66, Kennedy gathered them in the cafeteria and talked to them for the longest time, telling them what they could learn about themselves when they hit bottom. The mark of a real ballplayer, a real man, he told them quietly, wasn't what he did after a victory. It was how he reacted to defeat.

"Always remember when the season starts," he began, repeating the sentence they'd hated so much when he'd said it after their first win. But after a loss, it sounded awfully good: "The season starts tomorrow."

Tomorrow. The state finals. For so long, it had been way out in front of them, ten games away, then five. Suddenly tomorrow was today. Up close, it all looked a lot more frightening. What they faced as they began the regional competitions was just what Kennedy had been warning of all along—opponents they knew absolutely nothing about. Worse yet, they'd be playing on the other team's turf.

"We're playing *who*, Coach?"

"Akron."

"Who's Akron?"

"*Where's* Akron?"

Kennedy's brow furrowed as he scanned the list of regional competitors, searching for information on this school, the first of their tournament opponents. "Looks like it's way over in the western part of the state somewhere," he mumbled, flipping to the map in the playoff booklet. The boys peered over his shoulders, following his finger to a dot in the middle of nowhere.

"Oh, man," Amir said, "that place is practically in *Mississippi.* How we gonna scout 'em, Coach, with the game one day away?"

"We're not. We're gonna spend the next 36 hours gettin' ready the way we always have," Kennedy said, blowing his whistle. Everybody snapped to, running the plays he'd drilled into them for so long, but with their insides churning. When they'd faced tough opponents, they *knew* them. And what they didn't know about them, Coach Kennedy always figured out, somehow.

Now, when they had the most at stake, they had nothing to go on. They could laugh at Akron, saying it was a school in the boonies, but they had to take them seriously. If they lost to them, there would be no Birmingham.

Worse, they knew it was their fault that they were playing in their opponent's gym. They'd ignored Kennedy's warnings before last night's match against Montgomery County, a team they'd beaten easily three times before. "You always gotta be ready with an ax," he'd said, "to kill the mosquito." Unfortunately they'd blown off Montgomery as weak and lost not only the game, but the home-court privilege for the next round.

Now with no time to watch Akron play, all they could do was try to memorize Kennedy's litany of "what-ifs": what to do if the other team had a tall man; if they relied heavily on a strong shooter; if they played tight man-to-man; if they switched defense styles.

He was ticking off more possibilities even as they gathered in the afternoon to board the bus to Akron.

Suddenly, Amir walked over to Kennedy. "Coach, what if me and a couple of the other seniors rode with you, to go over some last-minute stuff about the game?"

Kennedy nodded, and Amir grabbed Darin and Damon. "The three of us are ridin' with Coach," he whispered as they followed him, uncertainly, to the white van, where Kennedy was poring over a big map of Alabama.

"I hope you boys got a better idea than I do where we're going," he teased, then burst out laughing at the looks on their faces. Damon and Darin sprawled out in the big carpeted area behind the driver, and Amir settled into the roomy bucket seat up front.

Out onto the old state highway they roared, heading west toward Selma and whatever it was that lay beyond—farms and cotton fields and cow pastures, they guessed. Over the hum of the car radio, Kennedy began talking about team communication. It was more important than ever that they talk each other through the game, until they got the feel of the other team.

"And another thing." He paused, checking the rearview mirror to make sure the assistant coach driving the bus was right behind him as he sailed down the highway. "You gotta remember that when you're playing in a foreign gym packed with the opponents' fans, you can't let their crowd become a factor. You know what I mean?"

"Sure, Coach," Damon answered, wondering if Kennedy knew that's exactly what they were afraid of. "You're talking about staying on 'em so hard they can't score and their crowd doesn't get in it."

Dusk deepened to twilight, and the talk turned to the starting lineup. Damon and Darin sat up on their knees to make a pitch for using two players they were convinced had won them their toughest games: Terrence and Amir.

Kennedy didn't say much, but he nodded his head, and listened.

"I wonder what they're talking about up there," Terrence muttered, peering through the bus window at the four figures in the coach's van.

"Probably strategy about the game," one of the other players answered.

Horace jumped in: "How much you want to bet Coach is laying some of his stories on those guys!"

"I can just hear him," came a voice from the back of the bus, hooting. " 'Did I ever tell you boys about the time my daddy whipped me?' "

"That's not the way it starts," someone protested. "First he tells the part about how much he loved goin' up to the church parking lot to shoot hoops. He's gotta go over that about a million times before he gets to the whipping part. Coach loves tellin' that on himself."

"Almost as much as he loves beatin' on us about those guys he coached in D.C.," another voice chimed in. "You know, those hotshots that were bums till they started listening to him?"

At that, Terrence jumped into the aisle. "Frank," he said, trying to mimic Kennedy's most weary, disgusted tone, "you know who you remind me of with your lazy ways?"

Even before he'd finished, the roar went up: "JOHN BATTLE!"

Back and forth they went about John Battle and the others Kennedy had coached, as the bus turned off the highway and began following the van down a one-lane road. "You think Coach did them the way he does us?" Horace wondered out loud.

"Killed 'em, you mean?" someone asked.

"Made 'em chant the man-to-man, stayed on 'em all the time about lifting weights?"

At first no one noticed the sound of gravel crunching underneath the bus. Startled, they looked up ahead and saw Kennedy signaling them to stop. The assistant coach pulled the bus over, jumped off, ran over to the van, and began gesturing and pointing back in the other direction.

"I cannot believe this," Terrence said, announcing what everybody could see for themselves: "We're lost."

They looked out at the blackness that stretched in all directions, then at their watches. It was past 6:30, less than half an hour to game time. Nobody said a word as the assistant coach wheeled the bus around and headed back toward the paved road, flying around turns until at last, up ahead, they saw a signpost that said "Akron City Limits."

There was no city, or even a storefront or gas station, but way off to the right was a long line of automobile headlights moving toward what looked like a school.

A moment later, they were screeching up to the gym entrance and racing behind Coach Kennedy into the glare of fluorescent lights.

There was no time to worry about the dinner they had missed, no time even to think. There was only the clock ticking toward seven and Kennedy's voice hurrying them along. "Get a move on, fellas. We got things to go over."

They began trotting, then running beside him toward the locker room. Kennedy whizzed past the bleachers, firing off last-minute directions. "I'm gonna make some lineup changes," he said, "gonna talk to you about double-teaming some of their tall men." Suddenly he stopped.

Above a steep, narrow flight of stairs was a sign reading "Men's Lockers" and beneath it an arrow pointing downward. They all stopped, noticing for the first time in five months something about Kennedy they'd completely forgotten: he was in a wheelchair.

"The locker room's in the *basement*," Terrence breathed, looking at Horace, who looked at Amir, who didn't know where to look.

"All right," the coach said matter-of-factly. "Y'all go down, suit up, say your prayer. Amir, you lead them. I'll meet you in five minutes under the backboard." And he was off.

"Everything depends on tonight," Horace told the team in the quiet locker room. It was what Kennedy would have said if he were there now.

"Yeah," Amir added, "we didn't come all this way to lose." They prayed once, held hands and talked, prayed again. And then it was time.

Up the stairs they raced, and out into the gym. And then, for one long moment, they stood and looked up at the fans. They had never seen such a crowd at a high-school game. People jammed the bleachers, spilled over into the exit areas, jostled for standing room by the stage—all of them taking up the Akron chant as their cheerleaders stomped across the court.

Quietly, under the far backboard, Coach Kennedy sat waiting. His eyes met theirs as they ran toward him across the court, and even before they were all seated, he was talking, picking up right where he'd left off.

"We're gonna go out and play hard, play aggressive, stomp 'em out early," he said. They leaned toward him, trying to block out the noise, listening for advice that was so familiar they could repeat it by heart.

But this time, Coach Kennedy had something else to say, and he said it slowly, quietly. "I believe in you boys. And you've got to believe in yourselves. Go out there like I taught you, be tough, be unafraid, you hear me? You've come too far to lose it all tonight. I know you're in a foreign gym, you got no fans. But you got yourselves. That's enough. Now go out and play some basketball!"

They jumped to their feet and charged out. Behind them, one last, shouted instruction cut through the din: "And stay in the man-to-man!"

The whistle blew, and instantly Terrence was moving, passing, keeping one eye on Akron's players, another on his teammates. His eyes followed them as they fanned out, and he sensed, rather than saw, each of them studying the opponent just as he was, waiting for an opening.

Suddenly Darin had the ball, took a shot and hit it for three points—once, and then again a few moments later. Boos rippled through the gym. Terrence felt the blood surge in his shoulders and saw his teammates quicken. Darin kept scoring by threes. Damon dived for rebounds. Horace kept going in for layups.

But Akron, with every bit of the same speed and hustle and twice the height, pushed back. At the quarter break they were three points ahead of St. Jude's.

"Keep on 'em," Kennedy urged as they huddled around him. And they did, but already they were flagging. Hunger, at first only a dim sensation, had begun to gnaw at them. Their muscles ached. Then came the sickening realization that Akron wasn't tired yet, or hungry, and they had a gym full of fans driving them.

There was nothing to do but push past the pain, run the plays they knew by heart, and tighten up the defense until at the half, shaking with fatigue, they hung on to a six-point lead.

When the whistle blew to start the third quarter, Kennedy sent in his "coach on the court," Amir, with instructions to "keep talking." And one by one, amid the boos and the taunts, they all found their voices.

"Just get the ball in my hands," Darin called first to Amir, and then to Horace, and then to Terrence, "and I can hit it!" Steadily they took control of the ball, and the game. They fired and hit, fired and hit, further widening their lead.

On the opposite side of the court, the Akron coach sent in a player who within seconds took a shot from so far outside, none of the St. Jude players believed he'd attempted it. It arcked high, sailed, hit the basket's edge, and tipped in. The crowd roared, and Damon and Amir looked at each other, then closed in on the new Akron player the moment he started moving. They suffocated the outside scorer into oblivion.

Akron fought its way back into the lead, but for the first time all season, St. Jude's was holding tight in the man-to-man. Pushing back the hunger and waves of dizziness that shot through them, Terrence and Darin and Horace drove themselves hard, edging past Akron by one point, then two. At last, with less than a minute left, Amir hit two baskets to clinch the game, 85-82.

The final buzzer sounded, and they fell on one another, collapsing in a heap in midcourt, their ears ringing for the first time all night not with the boos of the crowd, but with each other's shouts of victory.

When finally they stood up and looked across the court, there was Kennedy, gazing at them with that half-smile they now knew so well. They walked over, their chests heaving, and gathered around him.

He looked at the circle of players. "Good game," he said solemnly. "Good, hard fighting. You all showed some heart, and some hustle."

Then he put out his hand, and, one by one, shook each of theirs— Terrence, Horace, Amir, Damon, Darin and the rest.

They knew there'd be more wins, and maybe losses, on the road to Birmingham. They knew there'd be other games to fight through in strange gyms. But for this one moment, the coach looked at them as though they were champions.

"That's what I call playing basketball," he said. "That's what I call courage."

Nine days and three victories after the Akron game, the Pirates headed north, to Birmingham. They brought home the second-place trophy from the Alabama State Basketball Finals on March 1, 1994. Today, the young men who played for St. Jude's still remember that season as the highlight of their school careers, relishing every detail of every game on the long road to Birmingham.

But when they think of the coach who brought them there, they do not recall plays, or wins, or losses. What they took from Walt Kennedy had to do with much more than basketball.

"Coach taught me about hard work and discipline more than anything else," says Terrence Thomas, now an Alabama State criminal-justice major with plans for a law career. "I learned from him that no matter how much you might want to, you can't dodge those things. You have to face them straight on."

His teammates echo Terrence's thoughts. They now pursue careers that will take them far from the basketball court. Amir Green is a junior prelaw student at Auburn University at Montgomery. Horace Lewis, a freshman at Alabama A&M in Huntsville, plans a career in business finance, while Darin Irwin plans to enroll in Alabama State University next semester to study marketing.

Damon Childrey says that in the end what happened in that pivotal season in his life was all about love. "From being with Coach Kennedy, seeing what he had to overcome, just watching the way he approached his job, and us, I saw that if you love something enough, there's nothing that can hold you back."

For two more years, Walt Kennedy shepherded the boys of St. Jude's through basketball to manhood. And with each team he had the same goal. "Everything I know, all that I've learned in my life, from my father, my coaches, is wasted unless I can pass it on to these boys," says Kennedy. "That's what it's all about. Passing it on."

We must constantly build dikes
of courage to hold back
the flood of fear.

MARTIN LUTHER KING, JR.

ACKNOWLEDGMENTS

All the stories in *Spirit of Courage* previously appeared in Reader's Digest magazine. We would like to thank the following contributors and publishers for permission to reprint material.

Acknowledgments:

Bill Porter: Profile of Courage by Tom Hallman, Jr. © 1995 by Oregonian Publishing Co. The Oregonian (November 19, '95).

The Power of My Powerless Brother by Christopher de Vinck. © 1985 by Dow Jones & Co., Inc. The Wall Street Journal (April 10, '85).

Lesson of the Cliff by Morton Hunt. © 1985 by Morton Hunt. Parade (July 14, '85).

Christopher Reeve's Decision by Christopher Reeve. "STILL ME," copyright © 1998 by Cambria Productions. Reprinted by permission of Random House, Inc.

Rachel Remembers by Richard McCord. © 1988 by Richard McCord. Santa Fe Reporter (December 10, '86).

The Russian Who Never Forgot by Charles Kuralt. "A LIFE ON THE ROAD," copyright © 1990 by Charles Kuralt. Used by permission of Putnam Berkley, a division of Penguin Putnam Inc.

Two Words to Avoid, Two to Remember by Arthur Gordon. © 1968 by Arthur Gordon.

On Your Own by Sue Monk Kidd. © by Guideposts Associates, Inc. Guideposts (September '91).

Papa Was an American by Leo Buscaglia. "PAPA, MY FATHER," copyright © 1989 by Leo F. Buscaglia, Inc. Published by Slack, Inc.; distributed by William Morrow and Co., Inc.

Summer of the Fish by Jack Curtis. © 1978 by Jack Curtis. Gray's Sporting Journal (Summer '78).

A Special Sort of Stubbornness by Joan Curtis. © 1996 by Joan Curtis. Flint River Review '96.

Play It Again, Dad by Laura Sessions Stepp. © 1995 by Washington Post Co. Washington Post (June 18, '95).

Message From the Sea by Arthur Gordon. © 1961 by Arthur Gordon. Guideposts (January '62).

Against All Odds by Amy Ash Nixon. © 1991 by The Hartford Courant. Hartford Courant (March 3, '91).

The Littlest Marine by Jay Stuller. © 1987 by Jay Stuller.

Quotation:

Theodore H. White in Columbia Journalism Review (Winter '69-'70).

Alice Mackenzie Swaim, "LET THE DEEP SONG RISE" (Blue River Press).

Hugh Prather, "NOTES ON LOVE AND COURAGE" (Doubleday).

Michael Jordan, "FOR THE LOVE OF THE GAME" (Crown Publishers).

Clare Booth Luce in The Human Life Review (May '79).

James Baldwin, "NOBODY KNOWS MY NAME" (Vintage Books).

Charles R. Swindoll, "GROWING STRONG IN THE SEASONS OF LIFE" (Zondervan).

James Baldwin, "NOBODY KNOWS MY NAME" (Vintage Books).

H. Jackson Browne, "LIFE'S LITTLE INSTRUCTION BOOK" (Rutledge Hill Press).

Harrison Ford, "HARRISON FORD: IMPERFECT HERO" (Carol Publishing).

Bern Williams in The Independent-Enterprise News (Edinboro, Pa.).

Biblical scriptures are from the "REVISED STANDARD VERSION OF
   THE BIBLE," National Council of the Churches of Christ in the USA
   (Thomas Nelson).

Photo credits:

p. 112: Chris Ferebee/photonica

p. 117: Index Stock Imagery

p. 121: Gary Nolton/Tony Stone Worldwide

p. 126: Martine Mouchy/Tony Stone Worldwide

p. 128: Index Stock Imagery

p. 130-131: William Thompson/photonica

p. 134: Index Stock Imagery

p. 138-139: Gildo Nicolo Spadoni/Graphistock

p. 143: Bruce Hands/Tony Stone Worldwide

p. 149: Index Stock Imagery

p. 152-153: Brian Yarvin/Photo Researchers

p. 171: Index Stock Imagery

p. 174-175: photonica

p. 177: Index Stock Imagery

p. 180: George Lepp/Tony Stone Worldwide

p. 191: Jana Leon/Graphistock

p. 195: Index Stock Imagery

p. 210: Todd Haiman/Graphistock

p. 217: Jana Leon/Graphistock

p. 222: Todd Haiman/Graphistock

p. 229: Todd Haiman/Graphistock

p. 234: Index Stock Imagery

p. 241: Todd Haiman/Graphistock

Carousel Research: Laurie Platt Winfrey, Van Bucher